PRAISE FOR *MORNING SUNSHINE!*

"Your self-image is dependent on what other people think of you. It can be taken away from you at any time, by the good and bad opinions of the world. True self-esteem comes from going beyond your image and knowing the core of your being, which is beneath no one, fearless, and immune to criticism. Robin Meade's MORNING SUNSHINE! is an elegant journey from self-image to self-esteem. A book that will help anyone who wants to radiate true self-confidence."

—Deepak Chopra, author,
Reinventing the Body, Resurrecting the Soul

"When my friend and colleague Robin Meade asked me to read an advance copy of her book, I was honored and excited. After all, Robin is a beloved character by everyone at HLN and CNN. And, while we are very close, as I turned the pages I learned things about her I never knew. It is an amazingly candid and honest introspective look at her own life. Anyone who has ever wondered if they have what it takes to build their confidence or succeed at the impossible should read this book."

—Dr. Sanjay Gupta, CNN chief medical correspondent

"Terrific! MORNING SUNSHINE! is an excellent read. It gave me encouragement to face my own fears. This book should be used as a learning tool for many—but especially for young girls who second-guess their inner strength. I enjoyed the book and couldn't put it down."

—Jackie Joyner-Kersee,
three-time Olympic gold medalist

"Robin Meade is a joy to watch on air, and her new book, MORNING SUNSHINE!, will put a smile on your face and a spring in your step. Funny, thoughtful, caring—that's Robin, and reading MORNING SUNSHINE! is like sitting with her at home—listening to and learning from a close friend."

—Anderson Cooper, anchor, CNN

"Robin Meade doesn't provide just morning sunshine but all-day enlightenment in this charming book of love, life, and laughter. An instant pick-me-up, with lessons you'll keep with you forever."   —Sarah Ivens, editor at large, *OK! Magazine*

"I loved reading Robin's book because it inspired me, and I am certain it will inspire everyone who reads it. She tells her story with a moving and beautiful first-person narrative. She truly writes from her heart, and that comes through on every page. MORNING SUNSHINE! helped me, and it will help you as well."

—Wolf Blitzer, CNN anchor of *The Situation Room*

"Just like Robin on the morning news, her book is a feel-good positive boost of adrenaline."

—Sara Blakely, founder of Spanx

MORNING SUNSHINE!

MORNING SUNSHINE!

*How to Radiate Confidence
and Feel It Too*

ROBIN MEADE

**CENTER
STREET**

New York   Boston   Nashville

Center Street
Hachette Book Group
237 Park Avenue
New York, NY 10017

www.centerstreet.com

Center Street is a division of Hachette Book Group, Inc.
The Center Street name and logo are trademarks of
Hachette Book Group, Inc.

The publisher is not responsible for websites (or their content)
that are not owned by the publisher.

Printed in the United States of America

Originally published in hardcover by Center Street.

First Trade Edition: May 2011
10 9 8 7 6 5 4 3 2 1

The Library of Congress has cataloged the hardcover
edition as follows:

Meade, Robin.
    Morning Sunshine! : how to radiate confidence and feel it
            too / Robin Meade. — 1st ed.
        p. cm.
    ISBN 978-1-59995-164-5
    1. Attitude (Psychology)   2. Confidence.   I. Title.

    BF327.M43 2009
    158.2—dc22
    2009013078

    ISBN 978-1-59995-165-2 (pbk.)

*To Tim, for your humor, unconditional love,
and constant confidence in me all these years. I love you!*

*And to Dr. Amelia Case, for twisting me around
to look at myself. Thank you!*

CONTENTS

Introduction: *My Morning Sunshine*   1

1. Three…Two…One: Meltdown!   11
   Where Did My Confidence Go?

2. My Name Is Robin and I'm a Shape-Shifter   26
   Losing the Real You

3. Doctor, Doctor, Give Me the News   47
   Your Diagnosis: Bad Self-Esteem

4. I Don't Need No Stinking Help   65
   The Chiropractor with the Spine

5. Begin the Breakthrough   74
   Learn to Stay in the Present

6. What's on Your Pedestal?   91
   *The Difference Between Being Liked and
   Being Respected*

7. Stop Judging Yourself!   103
   Is This the Secret to Confidence?

8. The Bitch Is Back!   116
Let's Go on a Bitch Recognition Campaign

9. Be Yourself   131
Who Else Ya Gonna Be?

10. Frenemies   137
Feeling Confident While Fielding Criticism

11. Frick and Frack   155
Balancing Your Life

12. Breaking News!   163
What Do You Want Your Life's Headline to Say?

13. Your Passion Is Your Confidence   172
(Your Compassion Is, Too!)

14. Be Grateful for Your Gifts!   184
Are You Taking Your Gifts for Granted?

15. Your Void Becomes Your Value   196
When a Struggle Becomes a Strength

16. The Confidence to Be a Good Spouse   215
Introducing... Crystal!

A Note from the Author   233

Acknowledgments   237

About the Author   241

MORNING SUNSHINE!

INTRODUCTION

My Morning Sunshine

"How do you do it?"

The soccer mom–looking lady was leaning in sideways to peer into my face as I tried to print out pictures at the Kodak kiosk at the pharmacy.

"How do you stay so upbeat, even though you have to get up so early and talk about depressing stories?"

She tried to maintain eye contact, but I could see her eyes darting from my face (still caked with TV makeup) to my purse (large enough for a small child to hide in) to my pictures (oh, geez, what was I printing?) to my shoes (flip-flops from the craft store's summer aisle)—as if she were taking inventory.

Aha! What we had here was an avid viewer of the morning TV show I anchor four hours a day, *Morning Express with Robin Meade*, on HLN (or, as you used to know it, Headline News). And she had caught me right then and there, bathed in the unflattering lights of the corner drugstore.

"Well, it's not always easy," I replied, wanting her to know I wasn't immune to stories like the one stuck in my brain that day of a toddler whose mother had allegedly neglected for a month to even tell anyone she was missing. I hurried on, "But we have a good team around us who makes work not seem like work."

It's my fallback answer to common questions from viewers, such as: "What time do you get up?" "Is it hard to do breaking news?" Then there's the real zinger: "Is that your real laugh?" (Think more guffaw than giggle.)

But what I get the most is, "I love it when you say, 'Morning, sunshine!' Who is 'Morning Sunshine?'" (Even country music king Kenny Chesney recently halted my interview with him to ask me that question.)

If you watch my show, you know I greet you nearly every half hour of the show with a rousing "Morning, sunshine!" Sometimes news junkies think it's directed toward a particular viewer with whom they assume I have some special relationship. You know, the Carol Burnett I'll-pull-on-my-ear-for-you thing.

"Is 'Morning Sunshine' what you call your husband?" an older gentleman once asked with an inquisitive expression on his face. "My wife and I think you must call each other that." I theorized he and his sweetie had similar pet names for each other.

The truth of the matter is that "Morning, sunshine!" is something my preacher father would belt out in the mornings of my childhood, trying to root his three-kid brood out of bed in an uplifting way. It was positive, but to the point. Mind you, if that didn't do the trick, he'd rip off the covers. If you got a couple of seconds of the brisk air that still lingered in our Ohio home on winter mornings, you'd jump out of bed, too. It was a father's gentle way of saying, "*Move*, before I put a steel-toed boot in your butt!" He didn't have the luxury of letting his children make him late for his factory job.

Likewise, I say "Morning, sunshine!" to my viewers because:

1. It comes naturally after hearing it all my life.
2. It conveys enthusiasm about the start of your day—our day together—while being just aggravating enough to keep you from burying your bedhead back in the pillow.
3. People seem to sit up and take notice. Regular viewers request, "Say hello to me on the air!" So instead of risking sounding like Miss Sally in *Romper Room*, I tell them, "I'll say, 'Morning, sunshine!' at such and such time *just* for you!" It's a small way to make that personal connection we all crave. (And besides, I do have them in mind when I say it!)
4. It's become a way of thinking for me.

Let me explain.

CONCEPT ME, BABY!

If you move beyond "Morning, sunshine!" as a salutation, you can start to understand how to also look at it as a concept—*a way of life.*

Every single one of us has to find those tenets, beliefs, and mind-sets that sustain us and move us through not only our day, but our lives when the crud hits the fan.

For me, my morning sunshine is made up of many components, including:

My Husband's Humor

Tim does a great imitation of our fifteen-year-old cat, Ike, coughing up a hairball. He also makes fun of the Carmex I habitually keep on the nightstand in case the night air dries out my smackers. ("Mmm-mmm," he'll say, exaggerating his imitation by overdrawing his lips with an imaginary tube of Carmex.) And the dude will wager outlandish jewelry if I'll agree to do some outrageous act.

For example, "I'll buy you a GINORMOUS diamond ring if you jump into that birdcage and scream 'POLLY WANT A CRACKER!' for two minutes straight!" He actually made this generous offer at the World's Longest Yard Sale.

Honey, I sat eyeing the person-sized birdcage for a good twenty minutes, pondering how bad my jail stay would be. Because I *knew* they'd come arrest me and charge me with displaying a heapin' helpin' of *cuckoo*.

A Balanced Upbringing

You want to talk about *frick* and *frack*: my father wouldn't allow us to utter the word *darn* growing up, because it's a slip of the tongue away from *damn*. Yet my energetic and comical mother regularly made up her own curse words. I'd siphon worldly wisdom from her ("Learn to deal with people who act like asses, because there will always be an ass"), while my father spoon-fed us religion ("You *will* go to church three times a week") that provided a strong spiritual foundation.

Love of Family

Hubby Tim and I have yet to make a decision about having kids. We're neither for nor against it, we joke. But in the back of my mind I think, *Hell!* (Sorry, Dad, for cursing!) *I can't even make my dog, Rocco, behave! How can I be someone's mom?* However, the love I feel for my sister, brother, father, and mother (and don't forget the in-laws) extends to my nieces and nephews as if they were our own. If you were to come to our weekend cottage at the lake you'd see photos of Tim and me surrounded by them. One of my favorites shows the nieces and nephews nearly climbing all over Tim. He's grinning from ear to ear.

The Big G

Probably the biggest component of my morning sunshine is gratitude—gratitude for the things I can't control, like where I was born, to whom I was born, and my childhood. I'm grateful to God for the people I've met, and the places I've called home, if only for a short time (New London, Ohio; Mansfield, Ohio; Cleveland, Ohio; Columbus, Ohio; Miami, Florida; Chicago, Illinois; and now Atlanta, Georgia).

I've learned to say thanks for things I now recognize as talents but used to take for granted, like my speaking voice and my singing voice. Heck, I'm feeling gratitude for the blue sky under which I'm writing today.

My closest friend, Julie, whom I've known since high school, admittedly doesn't share the same feeling. She describes herself as having a "glass half-empty" look on life. I wish she could view herself as I view her. She's got this honesty that's abrupt, but refreshing. For example: "Robin! What's that fake broadcaster's voice you're using?" she blurted out when I was a cub reporter/anchor and didn't get that you should just "talk" on the air, not "announce." Julie is a talented businesswoman and embroidery designer with creativity out the wazoo. She's a loving mother. And very few people can recall details like she can. She's got the memory of an elephant.

I think she *rocks*!

She, however, somehow thinks she's less than fabulous, because she came back home to live and work after chasing her dreams in New York City. *Wrong!* She has so much to offer, so much for which to be thankful, and so much about which to be confident.

We all have!

Right now, at the drop of a hat…can you rattle off things you're grateful for today?

You can probably easily list the *big* things—your family, your job, your snazzy car—whatever seems big to you at the moment. But in my opinion you'll feel even more gratitude if you think about the things you normally look past on your gratitude roster.

For example, many days I'm grateful just for the energy to talk on air for four hours straight. Come to think of it, I don't know of anyone else on TV who anchors a show that long! So in turn, at this moment I'm grateful for my stamina and lung capacity. Not bad for a preemie who was repeatedly hospitalized with pneumonia until she was five years old.

I'm also grateful for my eyes, which allow me to see the camera and relay the news to you. For the Lasik surgery that allowed me to chuck my contacts. For the privacy and serenity I feel when I get back home. For the way the pillow feels cool on my face at night. For the air-conditioning in the sweltering Georgia heat. For the way the color red makes me feel. For the daily phone call I get from my parents ("Hi, honey, it's Mom. Your father says your hair is too long, and he wants to know if you went to church this week").

You see, it doesn't have to be big and grand, or miraculous and mysterious. We *all* have things for which to be grateful, for which to say, "*That* is my morning sunshine today!"

Even if it's just that you woke up today, *be grateful for a brand-new day, perhaps even a brand-new start!* Can you look past the negatives in your life and be grateful?

Confidence

Speaking of being grateful, I'm eternally grateful for the *confidence* I feel at this point in my life.

Con·fi·dence. So elusive, so abstract, so heavy a concept it takes a chestful of air and three syllables to say.

I haven't always been as internally confident as I appeared to everyone else. So how did I make the inside match the veneer of the happy-go-lucky go-getter?

To find and maintain our own personal confidence, I think we should:

- **Stop being delusional!** (That's right, if you're lacking in self-confidence you believe some things about yourself that are simply not true.)
- **Be grateful for things that suck.** (I know, that just sounds whacked.)

- **Acknowledge your inner bitch or bitcho.** (Yes, fellas, you, too!)
- **Find real balance in the teeter-totter of your life.** (What, you mean sixteen-hour days won't make us happy?)
- **Recognize where your void becomes your value.** Think of the stuttering child who goes on to be a world-famous actor. The woman who attains riches after struggling for even the basic necessities in earlier years.
- **Don't put other people's opinions on a pedestal above your own.** I think of the old line, "Enough about me. What do YOU like best about me?"

Isn't that a nice, neat little package of advice? Trust me, friend, it's taken a lifetime of desperately chasing people's affection (I read Dale Carnegie's *How to Win Friends and Influence People* in the eighth grade, mind you) to help me arrive at a place where I can stand confident on my own, regardless of my job, regardless of whatever my weight is that month, regardless of recognition (or lack thereof), regardless of the tangibles I have around me.

Hey, don't get me wrong! I love Louis Vuitton as much as the next label-informed woman! But I've got a silver-and-gold no-name purse I like just as much. It's as if I'm humming along at a whole different level at this point in my life, compared to, say, ten years ago.

Now, before you cue the theme to *The Mary Tyler Moore Show* ("Who can turn the world on with her smile?"), I should tell you there was a dark time in my career where *my confidence had wilted to zilch.* I didn't know how I got there, but I knew I needed to think my way out of the darkness. My livelihood depended on it. My life depended on it. Problem is, I had no idea how to hit the reset button.

Come closer. What I'm about to tell you, not even the head honchos at HLN and CNN knew until now.

Why would I divulge this information? Because I hope it will provide you with a road map of how one person redeveloped her self-confidence, got comfortable in her own skin…and kicked doubt's butt! And it may be a shortcut for you, if you find the little doubt devil lingering on your shoulder.

Forge on, friend! Turn the page. The story is waiting for you. And so, hopefully, is your discovery of your own morning sunshine!

Disclaimer: In this book, I'm sharing my experience with you. Obviously not every method will work for every person. But I hope even some of the truths I've learned will also help you!

1

THREE...TWO...ONE: MELTDOWN!

Where Did My Confidence Go?

"Thirty seconds to showtime," the floor director barked in a tone of voice that said, "Let's get this show in the bag so I can go hang on State and Division streets." I had just slid into my chair at the anchor desk for the 10 p.m. newscast in Chicago, cutting it close as usual. I squinted, trying to adjust to the bright studio lights. My eyes were dry from the long day that had started at 4 a.m., and my contacts were tugging against the insides of my eyelids.

The smell of microwave popcorn regularly wafted through the air at this time of night, as I plugged in my earpiece and threaded the microphone through my suit jacket with one swift motion. The popcorn aroma would make my mouth water. Yummy! My mind floated to Saturday nights as a kid when my parents would pop gargantuan bowlfuls of the stuff and we'd settle in for a night of *The Muppet Show*, *Love Boat*, and *Fantasy Island*. Now *that's* a weekend! (Friday nights were different. We were at the viewing mercy of my mother, who loved *Dallas*. If my father saw us kids gawking at the adulterous ways of J. R. Ewing, he would chastise Mom: "Don't be letting those kids watch that smut!")

If you've ever worked weekends, no matter what field you're in, you know the schedule has its ups and downs. On the upside, you get your errands done during the week when the stores aren't as crowded. On the downside—well, you're working the weekends!

The weekend shift was trying for most people in the newsroom, too. Most of us were happy to be staffing the widely watched shows. But the other side of the coin was that it usually felt as if we were working the grind, while the rest of the population was off soaking up what the city had to offer.

You could imagine the city's scenes: husbands and wives out on a date night, scarfing down Italian dishes on Taylor Street. Young singles, dressed in layers of Lycra, jogging along Oak Street Beach against the cutting wind from Lake Michigan. Packs of friends clustered in the United Center watching a Bulls game…in the lead-up to one of the team's many championships at that time. The theater district was humming with shows this time of night. Do-it-yourselfers were knee-deep in their weekend house projects.

…And I was nearly halfway through my grueling weekend shift. Frankly, I was looking forward to my head hitting the pillow that night.

WE HAVE INCOMING!

"Breaking story!" chirped a youngish crew member, jolting my mind back to the present. She breezed by with the scripts of the story that would lead the newscast. It was so late-breaking that the paper it was on was warm from the printer. Yes, ladies and gents: it was hot off the presses!

I silently fumed. *Why didn't someone come back to the edit bays where I was before the show and tell* me *we had a breaking story?*

Usually I could tell we had incoming stories by the crackling activity on the police scanners. My lowly cubicle was near the assignment desk. It was a drag to sit so close to the traffic of the newsroom when you were trying to block out the drone of inane banter or chattering police scanners. But the upside was that when there were breaking stories, I was *this close*, so I could listen in and soak up the information as a story developed.

Most of the time someone would find you, give you a heads-up that a story was developing, and get your input on how you thought it should be covered or whether it was worthy of being the top story on that newscast. You get the idea. But for some reason that hadn't happened this night. And this story I was about to deliver was news to me, too. *Oh well, maybe they got too busy.*

So there I sat. I was feeling guilty I hadn't shown up earlier on the set or been a part of the discussions about this story.

"Fifteen seconds," announced the floor director.

All right, let's see what we're dealing with.

I glanced through the script. First rule of thumb for presenting something on air you haven't previously seen or researched: make sure there are no "gotcha" names, pronunciations, or phrases that will trip your tongue before you even get started. (For example, *you* try saying "Russian president Demitri Medvedev" for the first time on air without a heads-up!)

On this Saturday night, instead of the facts of the story or the names of the victims, what I noticed ten seconds before the 10 p.m. newscast was the length of that story: *Wowza! That's a long-ass read!*

THE BAD THOUGHT THAT ATE ME

"Five seconds."

That news story was so long and layered that a Ginsu knife couldn't have chopped through it. With four seconds to go, I had a pessimistic thought: *It's too late for you to tighten this up, Robin. And you have no time to rewrite it in your own voice. Wouldn't it suck if you ran out of breath and couldn't make it to the sound bite?*

What kind of thought is that?

That's a worrywart thought. That's what that is.

Talking for four hours straight is no big deal to me today. I have to talk so much every morning I sometimes even get tired of hearing my own voice. (Kidding.) Actually, the show is so long I get an entire day's worth of talking in by the time it ends. I don't say a whole lot the rest of the day. Friends might think I'm not much of a Chatty Cathy because I don't yammer on and on about my feelings when they call. Truth is, I'm talked out! My personal phone calls resemble most people's business calls (just the facts, ma'am) because on the show, I talk and talk and talk.

But that weekend . . . so many years ago . . . something was different.

With my body.

With my brain.

With me.

Hubby Tim had noticed it earlier that day.

I was sprawled out on the couch at home, wrapped in a robe while on a break between two of the eight shows I anchored every weekend. (What a crazy schedule. It looked good on paper. And I *loved* it when I was off four days a week to make up for the marathon work schedule. But *during* the weekend, wow, that was a stinker!) Instead of taking the nap I needed, I was going over transcripts for a special report I was working on for the big "sweeps" month coming up, when the ratings would be measured.

I was assigned to find out which skin lotion worked the best at protecting the ol' epidermis in the Chicago winter. (I swear I didn't make this up.) It took me weeks to find a lab (in Montana of all places) that tested such products and could give me a quantifiable outcome.

Funny how, the entire time I was doing that story, people we tried to interview mostly wanted to share their "tried-and-true" home remedies to guard against dry cracked skin: "Crisco on the elbows might do it," a dermatologist told me. "My granny swears olive oil does wonders," one woman claimed. *But would I smell like pasta? Did it not have an aroma?*

Meanwhile, my husband was noticing my sluggish state

there on the sofa: "Why are you sighing so much and breathing so heavily? You're just sitting on the couch!"

"I dunno. I'm just tired," I replied.

"No, there's something else. You're not tired, you're exhausted! You need to call in and have someone else do the show."

"I can't just call in!" I shot back. "There's no way they'll be able to find someone on a Saturday afternoon to fill in for me!" *Wouldn't one of my coworkers curse me under her breath if she had to interrupt her weekend plans because I called in sick?*

As I said, I was a worrywart and regularly fretted over what other people thought of me. Never mind that back when I was on the Monday-through-Friday shift, there were plenty of random weekends where I'd be knuckle-deep into a pint of Ben and Jerry's, get the call, and haul off to work to fill in for whoever was off the weekend anchor schedule.

WHAT I'VE LEARNED: If you never speak up for yourself, you cannot blame your superiors when suddenly, burdened with too much to do or something you don't know how to do, you fail. You have only yourself to blame.

CONFIDENCE BOOSTER: Speak up for yourself. You can't assume that anyone else will notice how hard you're working—or that you can't possibly take on any more responsibilities—if you sweetly smile and say, "Okay!"

"Just tell them you're not feeling well," Tim implored.

"No, I can't!" I whined. Tim knew I didn't fib well. So why

didn't I just tell the truth? Well, let's think about it. How do you call in "exhausted"?

Such an excuse was run-of-the-mill in Hollywood. You hear of starlets getting hospitalized for exhaustion. But in a real-life setting that excuse was flimsy at best. Being "exhausted" was simply not acceptable. Not in my family. Not in the newsroom. Not in my mind. I would worry endlessly what my bosses thought of me if I called in saying I was too tired to work.

What if you get nervous and can't make it to the sound bite? The thought was still lurking in my head. Suddenly, it was as if it had invaded my body, too. As the familiar introduction music played, I may as well have been hearing the music to a horror flick, something like the DUH-duh-DUH-duh-DUH-duh-DUH from *Jaws.* My brain raced away with this new idea that I wouldn't be able to make it through the lead story, let alone the entire newscast.

See how my bad thought just kept growing and growing?

PLEASE EXCUSE ME WHILE I HAVE A FREAK-OUT

That night I looked down at the copy of the news story. My stomach clenched. My heart started palpitating. I think I held my breath without realizing it.

The floor director gave me the cue, pointing at me as the camera came up on my face.

I felt sweaty. Just as I opened my mouth to speak, the set seemed to fade into a gauzy haze. My breathing was jagged. The words came, but my voice was quivering so much it sounded like a kid singing into a big box fan on a humid summer day: "Bray-ay-ay-ay-king new-ew-ew-ews tonigh-igh-ight."

My hands shook uncontrollably, and I was huffing and puffing as if I were running mile twenty-five of the Chicago Marathon. These were not the controlled, measured tones of someone who had been doing this for a living for years. My heart pounded in my ears, and my face flushed. I was losing it, right there with who knows how many thousands of people watching.

What the hell is happening? As I delivered the facts of the story, I didn't hear a thing that came out of my mouth. All I heard were my own thoughts.

Oh, no, you're screwing up!

Oh, no, your bosses are probably watching!

You're going to get fired!

How will you pay your mortgage?

What will people think of you?

And then, of course, *Holy crapola, where is that sound bite?*

Can you see how the cause-and-effect relationship of my thoughts just engulfed me in doom and gloom? I couldn't keep my mind on the story. I totally slipped into imagining the future and the horrible repercussions of my screwup.

Because I'm writing this today, you can tell that somehow I lived to see the sound bite that evening. The whole looking-like-I-was-hopped-up-on-six-energy-drinks episode lasted only seconds. But it seemed like an eternity.

Now Josh, the I'm-going-to-be-a-reporter-someday crew member, and Michael, the I-really-want-to-be-a-rock-star prompter operator, were around me, wearing the same expression you'd have after witnessing a car wreck. "Robin, are you okay? Do you need a glass of water?" Josh's eyes were wide open, as if he really wanted to shout, "Dude!" He didn't know what to make of this.

"Yeah, please," I croaked. My mouth was cotton. I wished I had a trough to douse my head in instead of a tiny Dixie cup of water.

"Everything okay out there?" the producer chimed in on my IFB, the earpiece through which the producer and director talk to anchors during the show without the folks at home hearing it.

What to say, what to say? "Oh, sorry about that. Wow, that was weird! I lost my breath or something." I faked a half-laugh at the end of that statement for their benefit.

When Josh handed me the glass of water, I was surprised to see my hands were still trembling. I noticed how incredibly weak I felt, and I noisily gulped down the water the way my dog does at his water bowl after he's been chasing squirrels for an hour.

Get it together, Robin!

Miraculously, by the time we came out of the video and I had to speak again, it was as if nothing had happened. Except for feeling wiped out, I was back to sounding authoritative and in control, even tilting my head and smirking sheepishly as if to say, *You'll forgive me for that little freak-out I just had.*

THIS IS EMBARRASSING

The truth was, I was morbidly embarrassed—the kind of embarrassed where you'd rather crawl under a rock than face people. It wasn't the kind of embarrassment you can laugh off, as I could so easily when I was in high school show choir.

As the student body filed in for the Christmas assembly, I started jumping rope with a holiday garland. I was standing out on the gymnasium floor, and with each leap over the garland I felt a *swish!* After a few times, I realized the garland was catching my knee-length choir dress in the back and flicking the skirt hem waist-high, exposing my bum for the entire eighth grade seated behind me.

And laugh I did! Wouldn't you know it? The school photographer caught the moment: there I am in the 1987 yearbook laughing with my mouth wide open, my eyes as big as saucers, and my hands behind me, having just pushed my skirt back down.

I have no problem laughing at myself in situations like that. Take, for instance, my recent Humpty Dumpty moment at a parade in my hometown.

It was the one hundredth anniversary of the Labor Day Festival, and the organizers wanted me to come back to Ohio to be the grand marshal. The parade wrangler said they wanted me back not only because of my role in the public eye, but because I'd also been the Labor Day Festival queen way back when. "What an honor!" I said. "Of course I'll do it!"

Anyway, the day of the parade, there I was riding along at the front of the procession in a pretty convertible. Just then I spotted an elderly man who used to be my school bus driver. Back in school, I was his pet. He let me choose the music he played over the bus radio speakers, and he tried to take the bumps slowly if I'd conked out for a nap against the bus window on the long ride home. He even came to my wedding years later!

So I swung my legs out over the open top of the car, *Dukes of Hazzard* style, and ran over to where he was sitting on his lawn chair holding a cane. I then gave him a big bear hug, right in front of the crowd. Problem was, the next thing that happened was also in front of the crowd: I skipped back to the car in my fitted polka-dot dress, hoisted my hiney up over the side, and started to swing my legs over the top, as I had to get out. Except this time I fell back into the car, with the length of my back landing on the seat cushion and my feet flailing in the air. I must have looked like a fish flopping around on dry land! Every parade viewer on that block saw it. Not a proud moment.

How do you recover from that? I'll tell you what I did. I swung my legs back down to the floorboard, sending my head and torso upright again, and popped right back up on the back of the car, lickety-split. Just seconds earlier the crowd had let out a gasp. But now, as they saw me laughing with my hands in the air and my shoulders shrugged in that "What are you going to do?" position, they laughed and applauded, too.

You just *know* it's going to show up on YouTube someday. Oh well. At least I was wearing my Spanx. Ha!

WHAT I'VE LEARNED: Laugh at yourself before anyone else can.

CONFIDENCE BOOSTER: Become the ringleader, and signal that it's okay to laugh at your faux pas by laughing first. You immediately relax the tension and take away any ammo anyone else may have to make fun of you. Suddenly they laugh with you, not at you.

IT AIN'T FUNNY WHEN IT'S YOUR JOB

My point in telling you these embarrassing stories is that you can see I don't have trouble laughing off most situations. But my job? That was another matter.

No, I was not going to be able to shrug off the "breathing problem," as I had called it, trying to minimize its impact, even though it had completely bamboozled me on the air. It was all I thought about after the show, driving down the darkened streets of Chicago's Streeterville to our condo, still gripped with humiliation.

I felt as though every tourist lugging her shopping bags from the Magnificent Mile back to her hotel, every vagrant panhandling for handouts, and every pedestrian who called the city home knew I had just made a complete fool of myself. My brain should have been full of concussions, I was beating myself up so much.

How badly was I cursing myself? I didn't care to stop for my usual Cheesecake Factory late-night treat, let's put it that way. My stomach was still in knots. I didn't turn my eyes to gawk at the car pumping the thump-thitty-thump-thump bass at the stoplight, and I barely noticed anything around me on the drive home. I couldn't even feign a smile for the friendly doorman as I entered our high-rise building.

The ride to the thirty-seventh floor seemed to take forever. Every time the elevator halted and the door opened I held my breath, afraid the person joining me on the ride had seen the screwup and would ply me with questions.

Tim met me at the door. He had seen the "breathing problem" on TV for himself. I learned later it bolted him upright from his viewing perch on the couch.

"Did you watch me?" I asked, hoping he'd say, "Oh, I sensed a little glitch on your part."

Instead he just nodded, and I saw the worried look on his face. He didn't say much. He was waiting for me to go first.

I hesitated.

Finally, in the kind of voice you'd use to soothe a colicky baby, he asked, "Honey, what happened? Are you okay?"

I didn't know the answer. *Maybe it was a mild heart attack. Was it a stroke of some sort? Maybe I'm allergic and that was some kind of lung reaction.*

I was trying to kid myself. But mostly, I was mortified. I wanted to explain how I was feeling when it happened. I wanted to tell Tim nothing like this had ever happened to me before. I wanted to tell him I should have stayed home from work that day. I wanted to forget that it ever happened!

But there was no use talking. Bring on the tears, baby! And there they came. This was not the dainty boo-hoo of someone who feels a pang of emotion. We're talking bawling-so-hard-you're-funny ugly. It was like my favorite scene out of *There's Something About Mary*, where Ben Stiller's character walks down the street, snot running down his face because he's crying so hard, after losing his girl to Brett Favre.

What was poor Tim supposed to do with this blubbering mess of a wife? He took me in his arms, and I muffled my crying against his chest. Then I rested my chin on Tim's big shoulder and looked out at the expansive view from our apartment. If you had been there you'd have seen a direct shot of

Lake Michigan, dotted intermittently with other high-rises. The lights from the windows of thousands of other condos took on a starburst effect through my moist eyes.

Look at all those homes . . . with all those TVs on . . . and all those witnesses to my demise.

What if it happens again? I asked myself, mascara streaking down my face. *I'm so afraid it'll happen on the air again tomorrow morning!* I felt defeated, fatigued, and confused. *What's wrong with me?*

I hauled myself to the bathroom and chiseled off my thick TV makeup. I'd anchored so many shows that it was the third faceful I'd applied that day. With my face finally clean and free to breathe again, I hung up the muted lavender suit I had worn that night (and never wore again—the association with that disastrous evening was just too strong). Then I dragged myself to bed.

It was past eleven o'clock, and I needed to wake up at 4 a.m. for the Sunday morning show. I may as well have just stayed up, because sleep didn't come easily that night. The "breathing problem" just played over and over in my head, like an out-of-body experience.

What if it happens again? What if I can't do my job? What if I can't get up in front of people ever again? What will my hometown think of me? The people I went to high school with are going to point and say, "She failed!" Are Tim and I going to lose our home? Will Tim love me just as much if I lose my prestigious job? I wish I could think my way out of this!

The thoughts gave me no peace. They invaded my every moment, waking or sleeping.

It wouldn't be long before I'd learn I wasn't just having a "breathing problem." I was having a *confidence* problem.

The Takeaway

You've seen news video of a tornado that seems to be coming straight for the person holding the camera. Yet he seems frozen in place, unable to move or respond in a logical way. There will be days that leave you in a paralyzing emotional storm, like the person mumbling "Oh my Gawd" as the twister approaches. Just like the newschopper video that shows the scene from above hours later, time is the lens that eventually can give you a realistic perspective on your emotional turmoil. I've learned not to make drastic decisions about fallout from an unexpected event until a good chunk of time has passed. Like the objects in your rearview mirror, they get smaller the further away you are from them.

Robin's Ramblings:

Someone has to "make it." It may as well be you! You've beaten tougher odds before now. You can certainly do it again!

2

MY NAME IS ROBIN AND
I'M A SHAPE-SHIFTER

Losing the Real You

If you've lost your confidence—or feel as if you never had any to start with—then I firmly believe that you've lost touch with the *real* you.

Let me share a little of my experience.

Climb, climb, climb. Move, move, move. That was generally the way the broadcasting game was played. You start small in tiny towns, make big mistakes, and learn your craft before moving on to a bigger market for better pay. I started in Mansfield, Ohio. Little town. Low-powered TV station at the time. I toted around my own video camera, shot the stuff myself, edited the tape myself, and also delivered the stories on the company's FM and AM radio stations. Nobody was getting rich at that station. You did it for the love of the job.

Schlepping around equipment while toddling on my high heels was worth the effort: it was the single best learning experience of my career as far as the mechanics of what being a broadcast journalist require. I have thanked the general manager of that station many times for giving me my first chance.

Next up was Cleveland, long before any of us knew Drew Carey. "Hi. My name is Robin Meade, and I'm Miss Ohio. I'd like to have an information-gathering interview with the general manager." I really was Miss Ohio at the time I made that phone call. But can you believe I was so gutsy?

Fortunately the general manager was generous with his time, saw potential during my interview with him, and gave me an audition. Voilà! It was a big leap in market sizes to the city on Lake Erie with an economy built on manufacturing. This was the TV market I grew up watching, dreaming of being on the air someday with weatherman Dick Goddard and local news goddess Robin Swoboda.

I eventually left Cleveland for a better position in Columbus. It was a midsize city that seemed to sprout from the cornfields of middle Ohio. There were no local big-time pro football, baseball, or basketball teams to cover during the newscast, but you'd never have noticed. The town was so steeped in the scarlet and gray of Ohio State that an impersonator could fill his calendar during the party season if he could do a good impression of Woody Hayes, Ohio State's legendary football coach from 1951 until 1978.

By this time Tim and I were married. And we were there only six months, as I anchored the Monday-through-Friday morning and noon shows, wearing conservative suits that made me look twice my age.

*   *   *

And then there was Miami.

Wow! We didn't know *what* to think when we arrived. Miami had the dubious distinction of being the murder capital of the nation when we country bumpkins decided to settle in Aventura, north of Miami Beach.

Too often, the newscasts I anchored led with stories of gunmen targeting tourists. At the time, the trend was for thieves to stop tourists in rental cars, steal their money, and take more sinister steps if they didn't cooperate.

Our apartment complex featured weekly pool parties and seemed to be filled with parking valets and married men who kept their mistresses there. It was a pretty hip place, and we stretched our budget to live there. Picture it: by day we de-stressed in the hot tub, looking cool in our shades. By night we were eating rolled-up bologna to make ends meet. The silly decisions you make when you're younger, right?

You know what, though? I wouldn't trade those memories for the world. They taught me that Tim and I can be resourceful if we ever need to be.

Miami's culture, its mix of people, and the sexiness that we thought pervaded the lifestyle fascinated us. Yep, every new city was a learning experience.

MY KIND OF TOWN, CHICAGO IS

After Miami, I arrived in Chicago at age twenty-six to anchor the weekday morning shows at a network affiliate and do some reporting. *Heck, yeah—I'm ready for this!*

But when I look back now, I think, *Wow, what a kid I was!* The photo on my ID pass to cover the 1996 Olympics looks more like the picture of an intern than of a woman who would cover the Centennial Park bombing from those games. To me, my eyes look naïvely wide open. What I notice is that my hair is parted haphazardly and is messy from the Chicago wind. There's not a wrinkle to be found on my face. (A few days after that picture I got bangs cut into my hair, thinking it would allow me a more fuss-free 'do for covering the games. Wrong. They just curled up sausage-style in the Atlanta heat. Nice.)

Even though I was bright-eyed and bushy-tailed, I did possess the emotional maturity to recognize how fortunate I was to get a job in Chicago that early in my career. It was the third-largest market in the country, for Pete's sake!

In Chicago, I was about to learn more about myself than about anything else.

CONFIDENCE-CRUNCHERS AT WORK

You can probably tell that the news business is by nature a nomadic profession. And at the same pace with which I had moved from city to city, my bosses moved in and moved out, elevating their careers but forever leaving their stamps on the lives of the people who worked for them.

The nameplate on the news director's door seemed to change every time I turned around. It's not unusual. Chances are the same thing goes on behind the scenes at the station that broadcasts your local news.

Between news directors, interim news directors, assistant news directors, vice presidents of news, and general managers, I counted eight news honchos in the six years I worked in Chicago.

Each person had been hired to put his or her stamp on the newsroom, improve ratings, and do things a new way. So I tried to please each and every one of them to ensure my job and advance my career.

Every news head who walked through that revolving door was a different person with a different experience, and a different vision for what he or she wanted from the newsroom.

One might prefer a "run-and-gun" style of news operation. That might mean I spent long days of gathering news on the street after doing the morning show, to help make sure the story count was high for the afternoon shows.

Another boss might be into the "happy talk" on air that makes viewers feel they can relate to you. So I'd polish up my charm.

One boss wanted new videotape all the time. He banned replaying any tape on the morning show that had played the night before. Nice goal, but do you know how unrealistic that is? A very important story may *have* only one piece of tape. For example, in a convenience store robbery, police may release only a still photo of the suspect, taken from the security camera tape. It would be important for the community to see, no matter when they watched, to help police identify the perpetrator. Yet this boss wanted no tape repeated.

One vice president seemed obsessed with the hairstyles of the on-air folks. "We can't have you on the 10 p.m. news," she allegedly told my reporter friend. "Your hair is too blonde." So away my dumbfounded friend went, dyeing and darkening her Swedish blonde hair until, she says, it turned an icky green. Five hundred dollars later she was able to restore it to…wait for it…blonde.

The same VP also regularly corralled me for a verbal beatdown about my then-chunky caramel highlights. Never mind that one of the big local papers had just done a positive feature story about my hair, picture and all, and even interviewed my colorist! Fine, then!

By no means were these the only things the news leaders strove for. They all tried to make sure the newsroom delivered good journalism that mattered to the community. But you get the gist: every time someone new came through, I wanted to prove myself again and win him or her over. They'd each make decisions with what felt like the wave of a hand. Then soon they'd leave. The rest of us had to deal with the long-term effects of what sometimes felt like whims.

ARE YOU A SHAPE-SHIFTER?

Remember those *X-Files* characters who could shape-shift whenever they wanted? Yeah, I had become a shape-shifter, trying to morph into whatever was the going order of the day. I took every single piece of advice to heart, whether it worked for me or not.

Behind the scenes of the news biz are consultants whose job is to help you with your on-air image and delivery. And in trying to please other people, somewhere along the line I lost my *own* image. I wasn't comfortable in my own skin because I wasn't even acting as if I was *in* my own skin. I could adapt, and I did, yet I was just selling whatever role needed to be filled. At least that's how it felt.

Between bosses, consultants, and viewers, it got to where my head started to spin:

"Cut your hair."

"Grow it out!"

"Never wear red lipstick!"

"Your face needs some color."

"Give me more personality, razzamatazz!"

"I want you straitlaced."

"Talk slower than normal."

"Show me more energy!"

I would fill whatever prescription they wrote that was supposed to make me a good broadcast journalist. But I was losing the real me along the way. I was not being authentic to my true being.

WHAT I'VE LEARNED: One possible sign of low self-esteem is suppressing parts of yourself so you can fill someone else's expectations of what you should be. You try to fill someone else's (or your own) prescription of perfection, instead of being yourself and embracing your originality.

CONFIDENCE BOOSTER: Take pride in the things that make you stand out. Realize that you're better served by being authentic to yourself than by seeking out short-term praise from someone else.

THE MOTHER TERESA INCIDENT

Just this morning I watched an old blooper reel from my former station in Chicago. I looked at myself and thought, *Who is that person?* (I also thought, *Look how skinny I used to be!* But that's another subject.)

This clip is memorable for something I did and something I did not do on a newscast. It started like this: my coanchor announced, "And this just coming into the…newsroom." The camera was on a two shot, you could see both of us on the set. He continued, "Apparently Mother Teresa has died. This according to the news agencies in India." My reaction, clearly visible on camera, was to first look over at his notes. Had the producers forgotten to tell me about a breaking story? *Damn it! How am I supposed to ad-lib with him if no one tells me?*

On the tape you can see me peering at his computer to see if the info was blinking across his screen but not mine. *This can't be right. I don't see it on the wire services.*

My coanchor droned on, "The Nobel Peace Prize winner was to turn eighty-six today." No producers piped up in our ears to tell us he was wrong, so I let him continue as I searched the set for this elusive info that he was pumping through the airwaves for all of Chicago to hear.

Suddenly my mind flashed to the world's media, in town that week for the Democratic National Convention. I imagined wire service reporters, print journalists, and network anchors in their jammies, watching our local show from their hotel rooms. In my mind's eye I saw them jumping on the phone to their home bases and sending the info from this momentous report up the line for checking. I imagined what it would look like on the wires:

(Chicago) A Chicago television station reports Mother Teresa is dead. We cannot confirm. The source of the station's information is not known. World reports say she just celebrated her birthday. We are working to confirm the information.

Then my expression changed with the suddenness of a breezy day flashing into a windstorm. I realized what might be the problem: my coanchor misunderstood the producer's instructions to "kill" *the story* about Mother Teresa's birthday, along with some other pieces, because we were short on time.

"So to repeat," I remembered the producer had said, "Mother Teresa is dead," and she had gone on to list the other stories that were killed, too. Poor coanchor man must have heard only the "Mother Teresa is dead" part. And on he went, with a grim expression of concern and a voice full of sympathy, ending with "She has apparently died on the day of her birth."

If he had misunderstood the producer, I could not let him go on and impale his career. I could not let this happen to our show or our station, either. So I took a leap of faith and a deep breath and interrupted him on air, saying, "Actually I have a correction on that. I believe they are getting ready to celebrate her birthday…and that she is doing well."

I paused. Still nothing from the folks in the control room. They were probably too incapacitated—rolling around on the floor laughing—to reach the IFB button to pipe in.

I continued cautiously, not wanting to make my sweet coanchor look bad. He is a close friend to this day! "Can someone help us upstairs?" I asked for the world to see, wanting confirmation of what I had already announced. (Watching at home, Tim said it looked as if I were consulting with God when I said I needed to check "upstairs.") "Is that correct?"

Finally one lonely voice sounded through my IFB like a beacon in the night: "Correct."

I continued the cleanup. "She's in the hospital and improving. So we have a correction on that."

My coanchor kindly and humbly apologized to the viewers, and we quickly went to a commercial break to gather our composure.

Yet when I look at the reel today, my surprise isn't so much about my coworker's flub (it's easy to understand how directions get mixed up and misunderstood) as it is about my own demeanor. What I notice is how stiff and robotic I looked. I could have helped him so much more if I had felt comfortable in my own skin, and if I'd understood the value of letting you, the viewer, in on what is happening behind the scenes. Today I would just explain how that mistake happened—that we misunderstood the producer. But at that point in my career I was losing the real Robin to a cookie-cutter news anchor. I was trying to be something I was not: perfect.

ARE YOU UNCOMFORTABLE IN YOUR OWN SKIN?

"Don't furrow your brow!" I remember one viewer saying on my voice mail. "It'll leave you with a big, deep wrinkle before your time!" But I thought of my youth as a handicap; therefore, I tried to compensate for it. My brow was constantly pinched because I thought it gave me gravitas. Problem was, the audience knew better. I'm sure they watched me and thought, *Hey, you're twenty-seven. Shouldn't you act like a twenty-seven-year-old?*

So I wasn't doing anybody any good when I wasn't confident enough to be my true self. And I had no one to blame but myself.

But up until my career hit HLN, where I now work, I didn't comprehend the value in *being* my authentic self. There's a Sheryl Crow song with the line "You're an original baby/Like we've never seen before." Yet I was anything but original. I wore typical fitted anchor suits and had typical reactions to stories on air ("Wow, that's amazing!" or "Isn't that interesting?") After the consultants got done with me and I tried so hard to please them, I felt like the real hook of that Sheryl Crow song: "Turn around and you're looking at a hundred more."

When I look back now, I don't think I was wise enough or experienced enough to balance the advice I got with the real me. Now I can do that. If someone says, "Oh, golly, that shirt didn't look very good on the air," I can take that advice and not go through my entire closet and throw away everything that's the same color.

Can you do the same—balance other people's statements with your own opinion and what you innately know to be right for you?

WHAT I'VE LEARNED: Wisdom is learning to balance other people's advice with your own opinions until you come up with an amount of each that works for you.

CONFIDENCE BOOSTER: Put the advice you receive through a strainer of sorts. Ask yourself whether the advice will benefit you or whether you're adopting it because it will please the advice-giver. Being confident means never second-guessing the advice you accept or the advice you toss out with the trash.

DO YOU ROMANTICIZE THE PAST?

Have you noticed "time travelers" where you work or in your circle of friends? You can usually identify them by their moaning and groaning. They harp about the changes the new guy wants to put into place, or they'll romanticize the way things used to be. In short, they live in the past and fail to recognize what the present has to offer. I saw time travelers again and again in the office, resisting change and slowing down progress with negative attitudes. It's a futile effort, friend. And it could signal a slip in self-confidence if you can't embrace the present, and your present self.

WHAT I'VE LEARNED: Change is a constant, and it is teaching us constantly if we are willing to look for the lesson.

CONFIDENCE BOOSTER: Love the one you're with. Don't pine for the way things used to be. There is something to be gained and learned in your current job or social situation, even if it's only how you react to adversity or change. Likewise, don't be so busy trying to take your next step up that you overlook opportunities to learn at your current position.

That last point is similar to something I heard the then-executive producer of our morning show at HLN tell an intern. The intern was applying to stations for paying jobs, yet she hadn't even mastered how to write a factually correct story. She was so hung up on getting it written in a way that clipped along in a catchy manner that she forgot to make sure it was true. There's a sarcastic saying in the news biz: "Never let the facts get in the way of a good story." Maybe she heard it and took it to heart.

TUNNEL VISION

"Suck it up. Hard work will pay off."

In my cub reporter days I'd tell myself this, and Tim would remind me of it whenever I was at my wits' end from working long hours. Oh, I had ways around the fatigue. Breakfast was usually two Diet Mountain Dews and a Bit-O-Honey candy bar before the show started. (How's that for that caffeine and sugar jolt?)

Recently I ran into Jon Kelley, who used to be a sports anchor in Chicago and went on to work on the television show *Extra* in Hollywood. Jon asked, "Do you still keep a twenty-four pack of Diet Mountain Dew in your trunk?" The answer is no. But I used to, so I could grab one when I needed it during the day and to help me stay awake on the long drive home.

I had tunnel vision when it came to my goals. Come hell or high water, I was going to work like a mule if I had to!

For example, during my time in Miami I anchored the morning show and the noon show, and *then* I went out on the street and did health reports on things like encephalitis, virtual reality therapy, and little-known side effects of prescription drugs.

When I got to Chicago my station didn't have a noon show, so I would go out and do general assignment reporting after I finished anchoring the morning. Well, that's where you really get stuck, because my duties on the anchor desk ended each day just in time for the dayside people to start coming in and assigning stories. They'd look around, needing a warm body to go cover some story, not realizing how long I'd already been working that day. Some days I would work sixteen hours.

DO YOU ALLOW YOURSELF TO BE A DOORMAT?

Why is it we feel the need to qualify the word *no*?

Think about it. When someone asks you to head up the silent auction committee for the school fund-raiser on behalf of the PTO, you might answer yes. Period. "Yes" is your complete answer. It needs no "because x, y, or z." But when we have to decline, most of us feel we have to give an excuse. *I got it! I'll tell 'em my Aunt LuLu just got out of the hospital after gastric bypass surgery, and it's my turn to watch her lose weight!*

Then we spend precious time fretting over how the excuse, lame or not, will be received.

My coanchor on the Monday-through-Friday morning shift in Chicago used to say, "Robin, 'No' is a complete sentence. You just need to say no." Here's why he would tell me that: I was honored to get numerous requests for public appearances around town. Everybody from big organizations to little neighborhood clubs would ask, "Could you emcee our event this Friday night?" or "Could you do the starting lineup for our little run on Saturday morning?" And I always said yes. I wanted to be liked, and I didn't value my own needs enough to say no.

As a result, I would be booked from Friday night to Sunday afternoon and never truly think about the impact on my marriage or my energy level. I couldn't say no to viewers, and I couldn't say no to people in the newsroom.

In other words, I didn't have the *confidence* it took to say no. Instead, I shape-shifted at will.

THE INFAMOUS FRIDAY VAN INCIDENT

Take the Infamous Friday Van Incident, for example. On Fridays the a.m. anchors usually got to go home after the broadcast. But one woman had homed in on me to do a story she wanted covered. It was some promotional piece for a friend of hers. I'm not even sure what position this woman held in the newsroom.

"You're going to do this for me, right?" She had this way of peering over her reading glasses that made me feel like a kid in detention. Her eyes were like daggers. Frankly, she didn't treat me very well. So I wondered why she thought I should do this for her at all.

On the day of the van incident I should have been pulling out every excuse in the book to not do that stupid fluff piece. *Any* excuse! Like, "I have an appointment." Or the one that no one will question: "I have Montezuma's Revenge."

But there was that "Like me!" devil sitting on my shoulder. So I said to myself, *Self, this is a simple story. It will not take very long to shoot and write.*

Famous last words.

On the South Side of Chicago, our news truck started to spit and sputter. *Cha-boom chic-chic SHHHHHHH.* Finally, it gave up the ghost. That lump of metal refused to roll another mile. The other news trucks were out covering stories, so they weren't able to break away to come haul our butts back to the station. So we had to wait. And it was an all-day affair.

Finally, with my makeup melting off my face, I still had to go do the story once we got the replacement vehicle. It was a nightmare, and I said to myself, *Never again!*

WHAT I'VE LEARNED: You have to set boundaries. You must stake out parts of your day or week for things that truly matter to you. You cannot say yes to everyone's needs or requests. By doing so, you are saying your needs are not worthy of your attention.

CONFIDENCE BOOSTER: "No" is a complete sentence. But if you are prone to keep talking after saying no to a request, end your sentence with "but maybe next time." It allows you to feel as if you just offered a qualifier, even though you didn't. And it leaves the other person with an optimistic outlook about future requests. Let's be clear: I'm not saying you shouldn't try to help people. We all should. But you do have to draw limits for the protection of your own sanity and health.

I let things like the Infamous Friday Van Incident happen to me for three long years in that newsroom. And I felt obliged to work however many shifts I was asked to. True, that mind-set helped me garner more on-air experience, and a reputation for solid anchoring during breaking news. Yet why would anyone bend over backward to stay at work for hours on end?

It was like a drug to me. I loved the fulfillment it offered emotionally. On top of that, my thinking was: *I can hang in there, I'm young, and it's going to pay off in the long run, and perhaps I'll be promoted to anchor the afternoon shows, Monday through Friday, and finally get to sleep like a regular person!*

WARNING: CURVEBALL AHEAD

But then the station threw me what felt like a demotion: the *weekend* would be my new shift. Maybe it wasn't a demotion in other shops, or to the viewers. But to me it wasn't a reward.

The weekend shift was one of three problems that left me feeling pressured at that time:

1) Clashing Schedules

Working weekends meant Tim and I would rarely be on the same wavelength, let alone together. As he powered down to relax on the weekends, I powered up for a grueling two days of shows. I did the Saturday 6 a.m. and 8 a.m. news, the Saturday 5 p.m. news, then the Saturday 10 p.m. newscast. Then I'd anchor Sunday morning at six o'clock, Sunday morning at eight o'clock, Sunday afternoon at five o'clock, and Sunday night at ten o'clock. (I know, I know, what was I thinking?)

2) Economic Downturns

The weekend shift came along just as Tim left his job at the Chicago Board of Trade, where he had started as a clerk and moved up to being a trader on the soybean floor. Being a trader just wasn't a good fit for him. So he packed it up, came home, and started his own wireless wholesaling biz—right in the living room of our home. (If you've ever started your own business, you know nobody's getting rich for a long while. You're lucky to be able to keep the business phone line hooked up!)

Thankfully, Tim's intelligence and willingness to wear out the elbow grease resulted in his company's expanding many times over and being successful to this day. But at the beginning I was suddenly the sole breadwinner and felt the future squeezing in around me.

3) Cramped Quarters

We moved back to the city from the 'burbs and rented a cramped condo while we looked around for the perfect residence to buy. Our little rental place had bad energy, in my opinion. Or maybe it was just because we had two people, two cats, and two schedules all wedged into an abbreviated space. Duh!

But the biggest problem I had with my new assignment was that working the weekends felt like a step backward. I conjured up some ideal of where I thought my career should be…and the weekends weren't it. So I wasn't in touch with reality about myself.

Between the work schedule, the tensions at home, the pressures of bringing home the bacon, and my constant shape-shifting because I so wanted to be liked, is it any wonder I worked myself into a "breathing problem" on air?

GOT NEGATIVE THOUGHTS ABOUT YOURSELF?
YOU'LL ATTRACT MORE

The morning after my on-air disaster, dawn came early, as usual. I had spent most of the night sleepless, gripped with fear, worrying the "breathing problem" would strike again. I prayed it wouldn't. I prayed hard. And I again pleaded with my subconscious, thinking, *Oh, my gosh, please don't have another.*

The law of attraction plagued me after that. Again and again, at the start of shows, I had "breathing problems." They happened like clockwork, identical to the episode that had rocked my entire being the previous night.

The show would start, my heart would start to race, I'd begin to breathe hard, and my brain would say, *I can't get through the stories.* I even tapped my coanchor's leg a few times and motioned for her to take over where I had to leave off.

I tried breathing deeply, as you do in yoga, to relax myself beforehand. But even my hands tingled, the problem was so biologically all-encompassing.

One day a twist of fate saved me from certain collapse on air before a news cut-in. I was feeling especially fearful and thinking very intensely about not being able to get through it. In what seemed like a gift from God, the elevator stopped working, and the crew couldn't get from the newsroom up to the control room, so they canceled the cut-in altogether.

Wow, that was a close one! I had been just sure I was not going to make it. I thanked God for the reprieve. Isn't that awful? I was praying that I wouldn't have to do my job!

And the law of attraction was hard at work. The more I

feared not being able to speak at the start of a show, the more I could not. And with each one, my fear grew more intense and less rational.

It became completely terrifying and debilitating. Before long I began thinking thoughts I had never imagined would enter my head. I believed that after years of hard work and proving myself and moving around the country, maybe I had lost my talent. I had definitely lost my confidence. One day I looked in the mirror and said something that's hard to imagine now: "I don't know if I can do this for a living anymore."

Little did I know the hard work was only beginning.

The Takeaway

If you lack self-confidence you are telling yourself false stories about yourself and believing them! You've diminished your own worth in your mind's eye. The reality is, you have many abilities and many things to feel good about. But you've got to make yourself aware of what those things are. In other words, honey, you've got to take a good look in the mirror and see the fierce being that you are! The how-to is the hard part, I know.

I like what the Dalai Lama is quoted as saying when it comes to self-confidence:

Human potential is the same for all. Your feeling, "I am no value," is wrong. Absolutely wrong. You are deceiving yourself. We all have the power of thought, so what are you lacking? If you have willpower, then you can change anything.

Robin's Ramblings

Remember, big jewelry is gaudy only on other women.

3

DOCTOR, DOCTOR, GIVE ME THE NEWS

Your Diagnosis: Bad Self-Esteem

"It definitely sounds like you're having anxiety attacks."

That was the to-the-point, gavel-to-the-desk diagnosis my general practitioner gave me about my "breathing problem." I was embarrassed that I was in his office about this strange sensation that gripped me only at specific times, like at the start of a news show! (Whoopsie-daisy, that's a problem!)

"My hands were even tingling!" I said, hoping that if I described every nuance of what I was feeling, he might have an "aha!" moment and conclude it was a rare blip of some strange disease—curable only by a strict diet of cheesecake, pizza, and vodka chasers.

"You were hyperventilating," he answered, assuring me I had, indeed, been panicking. He made no mention of a cheesecake regimen. (There's a thought: cheesecake-flavored meds.)

Panic? Not some exotic breathing problem you can cure with a shot in the arm? This was not what I wanted to hear. The preliminary diagnosis embarrassed me, and it made me think badly of myself. *Anxiety? Isn't that a mental problem?* I envisioned a white building with LUNATIC ASYLUM emblazoned across it. *Am I a mental case?* In my mind, the stigma of what the doc was telling me hung in the air with a stench the whole city could detect. *What would viewers think of me if they knew I felt anxious? Wasn't I supposed to be the voice of calm, the voice of information?*

I couldn't reconcile my thoughts of what I was (anxious, unsure of myself) with what I felt I was supposed to be (authoritative, decisive, narrative). I failed to tell the doctor that anxiety as a feeling, not an attack, had pervaded other parts of my life for years.

NAGGING WORRY

For as long as I could remember, that nagging feeling of worry was as routine as the sounds of the ice cream truck on summer days in our small town, carting around its orange push-ups and red-white-and-blue rocket pops. As far as I can tell, I had no *real* reasons to worry or feel insecure as a kid. Although we were not well-to-do and went through some lean times, I never knew it then. My parents did their best to shield us from any budget concerns while simultaneously teaching us thrifty spending habits. (Hello, hand-me-downs!) We frequented the Fashion Barn in Sandusky, Ohio, for off-priced duds long before T.J. Maxx, Marshalls, and Kohl's came on the scene. And my mother whipped out her sewing machine and copied many of the fashionable outfits we couldn't find at the right price.

We had everything we needed, and regularly more. I had two

loving parents. (Sure, they bickered when they were a young couple, but who doesn't?) They both had manufacturing-based jobs, which were thriving in Ohio back in those days. And thanks to a big garden, my dad's hunting, my mother's natural talent for cooking, and a few trips to the grocery store every week, we always had plenty to eat.

COUNTING SHEEP

So why did I have problems sleeping at night, even as an adolescent? My brother, Kevin, can describe how I'd storm out of my room anytime past 9 p.m. on a school night if anyone so much as made the floor creak. "I can't sleep!" was the chorus that commonly rang to the rafters. I devised ways to drown out the noise of everyone else in the house: I kept a fan going, summer or winter, to insulate me from the ambient noise of the television, closing cabinets, or conversation. (It was my own "white noise" machine long before Hammacher Schlemmer made them, apparently.)

From the moment I got into bed to the moment I got up for school, I fretted about the bags I'd have under my eyes if I didn't get to sleep. That was especially true one junior high morning after a fitful night of sleep. As we hustled toward the school door, a male classmate whispered, "Ewww, you look tired! You got bags, girl!"

If you know anything about junior high girls, you know a misplaced exclamation from the opposite sex can have sudden impact. *Oh geez, do I look that bad? I gotta get some shut-eye tonight!* You can probably predict the result. Since I then had additional reason to be concerned about my troubled sleep, there were even more nights where I could not find peace.

DOGGY DRAMA

Why did I concern myself daily with whether the dog was eating enough? We had a highly intelligent and obedient golden retriever that my grandmother had given us. Champ was so well mannered, he didn't like eating in front of humans! He'd wait for us to close the garage door where he bedded down at night before he'd eat his bowl of food. It worried me so much that I spent hours trying to peek in a sliver of the open door so I could see for myself that our puppy was eating.

And why was I concerned with dying as a kid, wondering whether I'd go to Heaven or not? Probably because of the many hellfire-and-brimstone sermons I sat through, listening to my father preach at church. But you're talking about an elementary school kid here, overly concerned about going to sleep and never waking up.

According to the lessons I had heard at church, I hadn't been saved because I wasn't baptized yet, thus my concern. Once, when I was in third grade, maybe even younger, I asked my dad to baptize me. I wanted to get dunked—not because I wanted to proclaim faith, but because I wanted to save my butt from whatever I thought was going to get me in the great beyond. My father said no, apparently seeing my heart wasn't in the right place.

And why did I convince myself in fifth grade, even though I was a top student, that I was going to flunk? I dreaded report card day, even though I did my homework on time, listened in class, and did fairly well on quizzes and tests. I daydreamed what it would be like to tell your friends you were being held back while the rest of them trundled on to sixth grade.

You see, all my life, being worried about *something* seemed to be my natural state.

"IT COULD BE SOMETHING SERIOUS!"

What am I doing here? I couldn't believe I was in that medical office in Chicago, sitting on the crinkly white paper covering the exam table and telling someone who knew so little about me such a big secret! I could have had an Abrams tank at my beck and call and still felt insecure about my decision to be there, and about myself.

Well, what are you going to do when your parents are harping at you to get a checkup, after you told them you weren't feeling quite right? You know how persuasive mothers can be when they pepper your home with phone calls, using the same tone of voice they employed when you were a kid and kept forgetting to turn in your library books.

"It could be something serious!" My mother's voice got higher when she was frustrated and trying to push her point. "You *know* there are heart problems on your grandmother's side!" *Is that a stamping foot I hear over the phone?*

I could get my head irreversibly stuck up my ass, and my mom would still worry it was a medical issue of the heart. Clear that up, and *then* we can see why her daughter was taking on the tracheal habits of a Sleestak (those wheezing, hissing creatures from *Land of the Lost*).

Poor thing, my loving mother was worried and hurting for

me. Sometimes I wonder if she internalized every emotional pain she saw any of her children experience in life and held grudges against the people she felt were responsible for them. Like my frenemies. You know, friends who are really enemies.

"Those bitches!" she said, when I told her some of my frenemies from high school weren't coming to our twentieth-year reunion. "They probably didn't lose weight and didn't want people to see them!" That was her explanation for the no-shows. She's still ticked off at what seemed like constant torment from my frenemies when I was a teen. It's as if her recipe for relieving pain is a spell that ends with "Those bitches!" flying Tourette's-like from her tongue.

Now, the frenemies could have had legitimate scheduling conflicts or lived on the other side of the country, or maybe they just plain didn't want to come to the high school reunion. "Those bitches!" she'd still say. I think it's her small way of sticking it to 'em, even if she is just saying "Those bitches!" over and over.

When it came to my anxiety, I wished it were something merely medical that I could fix with one doctor's visit. Or maybe just a spell that ended with a curse word, too.

Nope, it was going to be harder than that.

THERE'S A MESSAGE IN THEM THAR ATTACKS!

With the benefit of hindsight I can see there was a message in my anxiety. But amid the hassle of having panic attacks I hadn't sprouted the antennae with which to decipher what my subconscious was screaming. It's as if the universe were putting up huge highway signs saying DANGER! FALLING BOULDERS AHEAD! Yet I was blind to them.

I sent up incessant prayers: "God, please help me *not* to have anxiety today!" "God, I'm begging you to release me from these feelings!" You may already realize that putting that much energy into something and dreading it constantly will only bring about more of the same. Think about it. When you can't fall asleep at night, you think about how cruddy you're going to feel the next day. As a result, you start to get frustrated and upset that you're still not falling asleep. And you attract more thoughts of not being able to fall asleep. Therefore, you don't fall asleep and end up waking up half-cocked the next day.

I should have been praying, "Help me see the message and the reasons for my feelings." Yeah, I know. Easier said than done, right? I needed to listen to my body and soul, but I didn't realize it at the time. Mine were throwing a royal tantrum, and still I wasn't hearing it.

WHAT I'VE LEARNED: The more you fear anxiety or bad feelings, the more they will show up in your life.

CONFIDENCE BOOSTER: The moment you stop fearing and dreading those feelings is the instant you give them permission to stop.

LOSING MY CONFIDENCE

So I continued to live what became a nightmare for me. I began to watch other anchors giving the news and think, *Wow, look at them, talking on and on, asking all the right questions, without even catching a breath! I used to be able to do that.* I'd sit and watch the evening anchor do a show solo and be amazed at it. Actually, I was more amazed that *I* had had the ability to do that before my episodes. It was a big reversal in my thoughts about myself, and clear evidence of how much my confidence had ebbed away.

I like the comments Tina Fey made when she won Best Comedy Actress at the prime-time Emmy Awards in 2008. She thanked her parents for "somehow raising me to have confidence that is disproportionate with my looks and abilities. Well done. That is what all parents should do."

My confidence pre-panic was probably disproportionate, too, but I used it to my benefit. Up until that time I had been the person who would put off writing speeches for work-related appearances until the morning of the event, then scribble down a few notes and deliver my talk as if I were the Anthony Robbins of news anchors. You'd have thought I'd had the speech ready in my back pocket for years.

At one particular event for the St. Jude Children's Research Hospital, I waited until eight that morning to even fathom what I would say to hundreds of people who had paid good money to be there for an extremely important cause. Sitting down at the computer and cracking my knuckles à la some caricature of a great piano player, I started to organize my thoughts. My face still had sheet marks across it, and my hair looked as if it had had a party after I went to bed.

Sweat it? Nah, I didn't sweat it at all!

You can do this! Piece of cake! That's what my brain told me regularly before I lost the real me to shape-shifting. I was confident I could speak from the heart and move the audience the way a good presenter should. So after deciding it was too late to write something formal on the computer I grabbed a few index cards, wrote an outline, and trudged back upstairs to morph into anchorwoman-slash-charity speaker.

Picture it: now it's 11:30 a.m. I'm at the hotel and a little surprised at how crowded the ballroom is. This is a seriously well-planned event.

You never know when you show up to appearances what's in store for you. Some are so well done that you get the scripts for emceeing weeks ahead of time, while other organizers have no idea even how the flow of the program should go. I recently emceed an event so poorly planned I had to help them decide the best way to get the audience through the buffet line before there was an all-points assault on the hot bar.

So there I was at the St. Jude event in my best church suit and high-heeled pumps—all that was missing was my "Jesus hat," as some of the church ladies call it—onstage in front of socialites, charity organizers, concerned parents, and philanthropic families.

Someone introduced me.

I started to speak. "Thank you so much for having me here today. It's an honor, and this is such an important event."

I wanted to launch into my message about a girl I grew up with who battled childhood cancer for years. But the back of the room was still humming with brunch-time chatter. It was rude. And distracting to the people in the middle and front of the room.

This is way too important a cause to have people missing the mes-

sage due to erroneous chatter. I'm confident I can get their attention. "People in the back of the room," I heard myself say, "you must not be able to hear me, because I can hear you talking amongst yourselves, and I know you wouldn't be so rude if you could hear the person up onstage. So let's check the sound system now. Applaud wildly if you can hear me and what I'm saying right now."

Well, the room erupted. People were snickering that I had the nerve to call the chatterboxes on the carpet. "Oh no she didn't!" was the expression on some of the faces in the front of the room. They were in on my trick to get the others to home in on my message.

And the talk-talkers in the room evidently thought, *What are we missing? People are standing up and whoop-whooping. Let's try to hear what's going on!* Because suddenly I had everyone's attention.

Silence. All ears.

Works like a charm every time.

Only a confident person could go out on a limb like that to get the audience in the palm of her hand. Right?

But post-panic, I'd spend hours marveling at what I *used* to have the guts to do and wondering where that lady went. It's our nature to take our talents, abilities, and situations for granted until they are taken away.

Only when mine were taken away did I truly become grateful for the public speaking talents I had! Isn't that just the way human nature works? For years it hadn't occured to me how tough it is to speak conversationally for hours on end, holding viewers' attention and giving them information in a journalistically sound way.

And I was only made grateful by the fact that my world was falling apart on me, thanks to the bugaboo of *anxiety*!

ASKING FOR HELP

Now, once you found out what the problem was, wouldn't you go and get help? And that's what I should have done. That would seem logical. But the fear that caused me anxiety was the same fear that kept me from asking for help! Talk about a vicious circle! I was so secretive only Tim knew the real terror I felt.

"Oh-oh, she can't handle her job." I was frozen by the fear that's what my bosses would say if they caught wind of my issue. I shuddered to think that the TV columnists in town might get a hold of the info and splash it across their columns.

Do you see how many of my thoughts became rooted in fear? I was letting my fear manage me, instead of my managing it. Look back at what I've written here. Notice the use of different forms of the word *fear*: *afraid, mortified, terrified*. No wonder I was exhausted, right? Constant thoughts like those wear you out and eat away at your core of confidence.

Check it out: when my general practitioner said he had a specialist I could see, I shook my head and said something like, "I'll watch for signs that I need help."

Signs? What was I waiting for, the *Hindenburg* to explode on my head? Once again, fear was holding me back. I suspected the nurses in his office might gossip about it, or that the doctor would leak the story, even though physicians are bound by a strict code of doctor-patient confidentiality. My mind zoomed into fear-gear automatically. Zero to sixty in no time flat!

Every time I thought about this, a movie started in my head. I envisioned a group of doctors at a cocktail party saying, "My patient's Robin Meade. She's psycho with a capital P!" "You are going to freak—*freak*, I say—at who was in my office today!" I could hear the *Hee Haw* Gossip Girls singing, "You'll never hear one of us repeating gossip/So you better be sure and listen close the first taaaahhm!"

OPENING ACT: SMILES, EVERYONE, SMILES

"You're just not happy unless you're afraid of something, are you?" One weathercaster I worked with pinned the tail on the donkey with that remark. Her comments stopped me dead in my tracks. She was the first person to see past the charade that I put on. And my troubles at work started to gnaw away at my home life, too.

"Things are great! How 'bout you?" was the play's opening line. Think of it like the start of the old *Fantasy Island* TV show where Tattoo runs up to the bell tower and yells, "De plane, de plane!" And then Mr. Roarke says, "Smiles, everyone, smiles!"

Poor Tim didn't get to take in *that* part of the play. That was for the general audience. No, I saved a dandy of a show backstage, so to speak, just for him: the cranky cuckoo dragon lady. Nice!

See if you've ever taken on this character: she yells at the top of her lungs while her head spins like Linda Blair's in *The Exorcist*. Then she jerks up the ringing phone and sweetly coos her best *Mrs. Doubtfire* "Helloooooo," as her fangs recede and her pterosaur wings retract beneath her dress. Yeah, her!

I can make it sound funny now, but it must have been challenging to live with me.

People who knew Tim and me as a couple then say they never realized my problems at work were translating to problems at home. If you ask Tim, he'll tell you 95 percent of the friction in our marriage stemmed from my frame of mind—the same frame of mind that led to anxiety.

But it takes two to tango, right? It probably didn't help that Tim had started running a company from our condo and was stressed about making sure he didn't become part of the statistic of failed small businesses.

Picture it: there's Tim in our home office, pulling an Al Bundy and waiting until noon to shower. While making calls all morning, he can't keep his train of thought because I intermittently stick my head in the door and say, "Can you come put this shelf together for me?" or "Drop me off at the gym, would ya?" or the trap of all traps, "Does this dress make my fat ass look fat?"

The little things he used to find adorable about me were becoming the flesh-eating bug of our marriage, because now he was front and center for *The Robin Show* every day, all day, during the week. And this show was suddenly a drama, not a comedy.

It flew in the face of my quip that "a little OCD does a body good!" That saying used to get a laugh out of Tim when he tired of my habitual ways. But now that he was suddenly getting a heapin' helpin' of it, it stopped being cute.

LOSS OF CONFIDENCE EQUALS LOSS OF SPONTANEITY

Oh, yes, honey. I had more rituals and routines than a pro baseball player.

You've heard some players will do the exact same thing game after game if they're on a winning streak. Many of them get superstitious. They think if they change up their pregame routine it'll ruin their streak. If you watch, you might notice a guy always touching his left elbow before he gets into the batter's box. Another player may insist on eating the same meal each game day. Grady Sizemore of the Cleveland Indians told me during an interview that he puts his uniform on in the same order for every game. He said he never changes it up.

Heck, we do the same thing as fans, don't we? Maybe you've heard your brother attribute his favorite team's win to the "lucky T-shirt" he wore in the stands at that game. So week after week, game after game, he'll insist on wearing the same pit-stained sweat catcher, even if it's so dirty it can stand on its own ("Don't wash it! You'll wash the mojo right out of it!").

I'm like that, going through the same drill before every single show. If you had a bird's-eye view, you'd spot two cough drops I keep on the set. One is in my mouth immediately before the show starts, to coat my throat before four hours of talking. I keep the other one in case I finish the first. You'll also notice a coffee cup on the desk. That's full of hot water to give my voice a quick warm-up, and to warm up my body. (It's usually frickin' cold on the set, to keep the equipment from overheating the studio.)

I also have papers covering the monitor that shows our competition and what they're airing. (I don't want to give the other morning shows my mental energy. Unless, of course, there's a breaking story and I want to see if the other guys have it!)

And what else? Let's see, I take two melatonin pills each night before bed to help me sleep. My current food kick is bagels and peanut butter every day before the show.

I realize having a routine is not highly unusual. We are all creatures of habit. But Lawdy, back in the "Where'd My Confidence Go?" years, as I'll call them, I went full tilt. My habits became hang-ups. My rituals became requirements.

I had to have a tube of toothpaste by the bed in case I woke up with bad breath. (Which I did often, because I slurped down four or five Diet Mountain Dews at work and dehydrated myself with all that caffeine. That twelve-ounce nutrition would leave me cotton-mouthed in the middle of the night.) The toothpaste had a lot of company on my bedside table: let's start with a beanbag eye pouch to keep the light out of my eyes, because I go to bed before it's dark outside. There was also a back relaxer that looked like a jump rope, but with little wooden wheels on it. If I couldn't sleep, I used it to rub my back and relax. I had Carmex lip balm on the table, too, and it always had to be there, because if my nose was plugged up, I would breathe through my mouth and parch my lips. (Tim said I used so much Carmex that I looked as if somebody had waxed me down.) I had to have a big glass of water and all my vitamins there, and I took a slew of them, especially B vitamins and calcium, because I'd heard they had calming properties.

There were other calming agents I had to have, too. I had a static noisemaker going all the time, and I also had to make sure I had Celestial Seasonings chamomile tea, because it was supposed to be relaxing. Poor Tim! If I found we hadn't bought enough of it, I'd send him to the grocery store at the last minute. It was like an emergency: "Oh, my gosh, I have to have my tea!"

In fact, there were some things that I absolutely *had* to have all the time, and I could not be without them. My underlying fear was that if I didn't have them, the anxiety might return like a thief in the night. I just got all worked up.

At one point I even had a taser gun. Why? I would go to sleep so early, and Tim wasn't always home from work yet. So I got a taser gun and put *that* on the bedside table, too. That way, if anyone ever came in the house I could zap him!

Well, you can see what was happening. It continued to build. And that carried over into almost every aspect of my life. Everything had to be the same, and perfect, because I was desperate to maintain control. The assumption was that if I could control my routine, maybe somehow I could better control my anxiety, and my bad feelings wouldn't return. In other words, if I could not control my feelings of anxiety and loss of confidence, at least I could spiff up other aspects of my life to the point of perfection.

TIME FOR A CHANGE

Well, after two drawn-out years of anxiety, loss of confidence, and my continually growing habitual routines, Tim had just had it. "This is ridiculous, Robin!" he bellowed one day as we got into an ugly, loud, curse-riddled argument. "Enough is enough! You've got to do something about this!"

I didn't blame him. I was a royal bitch at home because I was so unhappy. My "cool" job was no longer fun at any level for him or for me, and our competing schedules had us knocking heads. And now some worry-obsessed lady was looking at him from where his carefree, confident, happy wife used to be.

Since I couldn't think my way out of it, Tim was the one who took action. He went to his chiropractor to help me.

His *chiropractor*? That's what I thought, too. But keep reading. You gotta check out the way this woman cracked, twisted, bent, and flexed every thought I had about myself, without ever laying a hand on me. And in doing so she helped me find my confidence and my true self again.

WHAT I'VE LEARNED: Most of the time help doesn't come in the form that you expect. And it may not arrive on the schedule you think it should.

CONFIDENCE BOOSTER: Keep an open mind about who is qualified to assist you in your growth. Titles can tell you a lot about a person's area of expertise. But they don't tell you much about the person. Sometimes, the person who can most affect your self-confidence is the one who believes you can move mountains and convinces you of the same.

The Takeaway

Help can come in so many different forms. But none of it will work unless you're willing to help yourself. And none of it will help unless you're willing to work on it. One conversation won't do it. One pill probably won't do. It takes work, and a willingness to look at facets of your being you would rather tuck away.

Robin's Ramblings

Shoot for the moon. Even if you miss, you'll land among the stars.

4

I DON'T NEED NO STINKING HELP

The Chiropractor with the Spine

Here's the backstory (hardee-har-har) of the chiropractor who had the backbone to twist me around to look at myself.

Tim was a devotee of back-crackers. (Note: I say "back-cracker" in jest. I have immense respect for the people who help us align physically and mentally.) A star running back at Ashland University, Tim had taken years of hard knocks. (His hometown fans called him Tonka for the way he barreled through opposing lines.) His junior year, he was having the best game of his college career when his knee got blown out in a painful helmet hit by an opposing player.

I hadn't met Tim yet, even though he was Joe Jock on campus. I was a TV/radio geek during those years, as that was my major: radio/television production, programming, and performance. If you were a devoted radio/television major, your life revolved around the live shows that were produced and staffed every weekday on the college television station. It was shown in something like nine surrounding towns. As a result of the time it took to fill the part of the boob tube for which we were responsible, there wasn't much time for anyone or anything else. The TV studio was my sorority house. The news team was my crew.

Once Tim and I did meet, it was obvious to me how devastating that football injury had been. It was career-ending, and left Tim *this close* to an amputation directly afterward. Years later it required a second operation called a tibial osteotomy, where they slice through your leg bone, basically. The outcome is that one of Tim's legs is slightly shorter than the other. That messes up his back. And some days (not every day, thankfully) he can hardly walk. "If I could go back, I'd still play football, regardless of the aches it causes me now," Tim says. He thinks being a football player helped make him what he is.

A young man in an old man's body. That's what *I* say he is.

And that's where the chiropractors come in.

ENTER DR. CASE

In Chicago his chiropractor was Dr. Amelia Case. But Dr. Case does far more than align bones and dispense advice on how to soothe sore muscles. She is the chief of staff of the Universal Health Institute, which she founded, and a specialist in helping people change damaging thoughts and behaviors.

Tim remembered Dr. Case saying something about counseling people through "breakthroughs." *What are those?* he wondered. Dr. Case studied the philosophy of healing under the guidance of a man named John Demartini (you might recognize his name as that of one of the experts from the DVD *The Secret*). Eventually Dr. Case became a teacher of his methodology, and today she teaches it around the world.

Something about the way Dr. Case mentored people made Tim think this "breakthrough" thing might be just what I needed to help "break through" the chains of anxiety.

She'd been telling him about some people she'd helped out in the past with transformations, focusing on the vibes each one of us gives off through negative attitudes or judgmental views. This kind of work piqued Tim's interest. And he took a leap of faith, lying there on the table one day with Dr. Case stretching and manipulating his back. "Would you mind talking to my wife sometime?" he asked. He knew he was treading on dangerous ground by telling anybody what I struggled with, so all he initially said was, "Robin's really stressed at work."

That afternoon he came home and said, "Hey, you know, it just so happens that Dr. Case helps people with breakthroughs."

"Yeah, so?" I hoped a disinterested response would end his current "let's get you help" tangent. But it didn't.

"C'mon, Robin, please. Just go in and meet with her. Don't you want to feel better?"

"No, I can't do that. I don't want anybody else knowing. What if she tells people? Besides, what does a chiropractor know about my breathing problems?"

*   *   *

A short while later, I arrived at a decision that shocks me now: after a brutal day at work, I found myself giving up. I was emphatic with Tim that I just didn't think I could do my job anymore. "I don't love it like I used to." I let that soak in for effect.

Tim was quiet for a minute.

When he finally spoke, it was with resolve. "If you truly mean that, I'm okay with it. But I know who you are, what you are, and I know your drive. And I know you're not done yet. You will not be happy with yourself years from now if you quit."

He just wanted me to fight it, of course, but instead I fought *him*.

"No, I really *am* done. I hate my job. I hate what I'm doing. I'm finished." I allowed the shade of anxiety to tinge my view of everything at work. I had fallen into a negative way of thinking (the holistic-type people describe it as "a low-vibration energy pattern"), and it affected the way I saw my abilities, my purpose, my marriage, and myself.

If I had quit at that point, I still would have been very successful. Not many people get to the third-largest market in the country. But Tim knows that I set my goals high, that I don't stop until I hit them or die trying. And, of course, I hadn't achieved all my goals. The brass ring was always an anchor position at the national level.

OKAY, I MIGHT BE A LITTLE FRIGHTENED

Tim knew as well as I did that my quitting my job was not a financial option. He had just started his business, fueled by the hope that if he had his own company he wouldn't have to constantly give up his jobs to chase after me as I moved around the country from market to market. But in the late nineties he had no guarantees of anything. No guarantees his company would work or of what it could generate monthly. And no matter what he was saying to me, deep down he was shaken.

About a week after I told him I wanted to quit my career, Tim went in without telling me and set up an appointment with Dr. Case. Looking back, he says he *had* to do it, that he felt he had to save me. And it wasn't even about resurrecting my career. It was about helping me overcome my fear, helping me find my confidence again, helping me find the old Robin.

He knew how resistant I'd be to this, so when he talked with Dr. Case he asked, "Would you do me a favor and meet over at our house the first time?" Her office was actually about four blocks down the street from us in downtown Chicago. She agreed, and Tim just marched on home and laid it out to me: "Tomorrow at 5 o'clock, you have an appointment with Dr. Case."

UH-MUH-GAW!

That's when the shih tzu hit the fan!

I should have found all kinds of things to be grateful about at that moment. I should have been grateful for a husband who loved me enough to try to help me out. I should have been grateful for a doctor close by who might have the answer to what was happening to me. I should have been grateful for anything and everything!

Shoulda woulda coulda.

I laser-beamed in on what I saw as the negatives:

- Tim had betrayed my trust by letting the cat out of the bag.
- This woman was a chiropractor, not a psychologist.
- I didn't have time to talk for hours on end to find a solution!
- Other people might find out now!

So I planted my feet firm and said, "I'm not going in."

Tim had ice in his veins. "I know you're not. You're going to sit right *here* and talk to her."

Huh? Right here? That little sneak threw me for a loop by arranging it so I didn't have to be seen around the doctor's office. I had to quickly rethink my argument.

"I'm not going to be here," he continued, "so you can just be completely open with her. You don't have to worry about what I hear. It's between you two."

Score one for Tim.

Well, I didn't really know what to say. Finally I let my guard down, if only a bit. "All right," I said. "But I'm telling you, it's not going to help."

LET THE OPERATION COMMENCE!

Dr. Case came over to our place the next day. We went downstairs to the first floor and hung out on our big couches, and wow, it was intense! That first meeting lasted hours.

I found all kinds of ways to manifest my resistance to looking inward. Actually, I became an escape artist during these first meetings. Just as we started doing any deep thinking, my brain started telling my body all kinds of ways to get out of this. I had to use the bathroom incessantly. I kept feeling as if I needed a nap. My nose started to run. I'd say, "Damn, I'm thirsty. Do you want something to drink?" or "Oh-oh, I think one of the cats has diarrhea!"

When I finally settled down, we talked a lot about balance, and chaos versus calm.

I was apparently full of chaos. My panic was a sign of it. But, Dr. Case said, I'd find the calm once I got balanced in my way of thinking—not only about myself, but about all the things around me.

Chaos, calm, balance. Okay, I can grasp that. This ain't so bad, telling this lady my problems. And as she talked, prodding me with questions, all I could think was, *What a relief! This woman isn't judging me. She's not saying I'm good or bad. And she doesn't even watch me on TV!* I literally could have cried with joy.

WHAT I'VE LEARNED: Our lives fluctuate constantly between chaos and calm. The chaos, as uncomfortable as it is, causes us to grow and learn about ourselves. The calm periods of our life allow us to rest before our next learning period.

CONFIDENCE BOOSTER: When a challenge in your life leaves you feeling full of chaos, recognize that you've made it through chaotic moments before...and your memory of calm periods is your proof of that. It's like the breathless feeling of clambering to the top of a mountain...then taking in all the beauty the vista offers, while recognizing you'll have to hike through the valleys to get to the next peak.

The Takeaway

You may not have full-blown feelings of panic the way I did on the air, but who among us doesn't wrestle with anxiety and doubt of one kind or another? I let my ego stifle me at first by refusing to admit I was stuck in my own trouble. It's courageous to tell somebody you want something different, especially if you don't know how to get it yourself. Growth is intensely challenging because it pushes our buttons and makes us look at ourselves in ways we might not really like. And of course we can't do it alone. We have to subordinate ourselves to others, which means taking risks. Women, especially, are trained to be so subjective—*How do I look? How do I feel?*—that they don't always look at themselves from the outside. It's uncomfortable, even threatening. But the bravery it takes to analyze yourself objectively pays off in ways you can only begin to imagine.

Robin's Ramblings

It's better to be talked about than to be forgotten. (In other words, if you are the subject of gossip or speculation, enjoy it! Don't let someone else's negative energy control you!)

5

BEGIN THE BREAKTHROUGH

Learn to Stay in the Present

From the moment Dr. Case showed up at our door, I prayed she would give me the insight I needed to think my way out of anxiety. Little by little I began to reveal things to her that I'd held so tightly inside me for so long—things that were choking the life out of me.

I felt that I wasn't allowed to show my true personality on the air, I told Dr. Case, and that's what I felt had led to my anxiety.

For example, I used to have dreams when I anchored in Miami about being caught and scrunched in a box on the set of the TV studio, and I couldn't break my way out no matter how hard I pounded on the wall. (I also had another recurring nightmare: the teleprompter was all in Japanese. But that's another story!)

As I recounted these things to Dr. Case, I thought maybe my psyche and true personality had been boxed in for years by the notion that I had to talk a certain way, act a certain way, and look a certain way to be a credible journalist. Because I felt boxed in, or pigeonholed, I had a hunch my body was having what we eventually labeled as my "purpose attacks." In other words, I told her, it was as if my subconscious were saying, "Hello, hello, listen to me! I'm your body! You're not being treated as yourself here! You *will* listen to me!"

You know that life isn't all about work, but unfortunately, up until that point, a lot of it had been for me. Reporting stories, writing scripts, and anchoring the news were like drugs for me. Like an addict, I would go all day without food until I got home. I felt the rush of the responsibilities that came with my job. I wanted very much to do a service for the public and in turn have them like me. No, love me!

HAVE YOU SEEN MY INNER BITCH?

"Hi, sweetie." That was the greeting I usually got in the newsroom. My coworkers probably called me that because I had a reputation for saying "Sure" when asked to do extra shows. It wasn't a bad thing to be called, when you think about it. Better than being called "bee-yatch," at least in my mind back then.

When I wasn't at work, I was still afraid and confused. I wasn't totally sure who I was trying to be, or whom I was supposed to please. Was I really this goody two-shoes and "sweetie" people called me at work?

I was raised to be accountable for my actions. I certainly tried to act like a sweetie. I remember how embarrassed I was if anyone in Chicago or Miami or Cleveland ever caught me with a glass of wine at dinner. That was probably because of my upbringing, since my evangelical minister father looks down upon such things.

"I thought you stayed home and prayed all the time!" one of my coworkers blurted out when Tim and I met up with the news team at a restaurant bar. And the teasing continued: "Oh my gosh! I didn't know you went out! What's in your cup?" Seems my goody-two-shoes reputation had preceded me that night.

I was so afraid people would think I was bad! So I figured, *I must be good because people think I am.* So I was over-the-top sweet and didn't embrace the parts of me that definitely *weren't* sweet. I denied the part of me that has a backbone, the part of me that is competitive, and the part of me that gets satisfaction at saying a curse word under her breath.

We all have an inner bitch. But I wasn't embracing mine! By adhering to my unbalanced thinking that I was only a sweetie, I was not expressing all the facets of my being.

I'm reminded of a cute saying one of our makeup artists at CNN Center in Atlanta uses. If you get her riled up over something, she'll warn you before things get out of control: "There's a little redneck girl who lives inside me. You don't want to make that little redneck girl come out! You will not *like* that little redneck girl!" It's sort of the Southern way of saying, *Incredible Hulk*–style, "Don't make me angry. You wouldn't like me when I'm angry." Very effective!

SEE YOUR OWN BLIND SPOTS

Mihaly Csikszentmihalyi (how'd you like to see the pronunciation for that one spelled out on the teleprompter? Yowza) is one of the leading researchers on consciousness, and he wrote the book *Flow: The Psychology of Optimal Experience.* One of the things he discovered when he studied the optimal experience of the human being—meaning the body *and* mind—was that it's important to see yourself as an individual, but also as a part of something. It makes you better able to have a unique and optimal experience.

Dr. Case explained that the questions she would use with me would make my mind stretch around myself in a sort of three-dimensional way.

It's weird to say this, but the questions are devised to *make you see your own blind spots.* The Demartini Method, the method on which her questions are based, is considered a holistic approach. It's often used in a corporate environment. Dr. Case uses it in the context of health care, in terms of a living, breathing human being expressing his health and life through his actions and body. She explained that my panic attacks were manifestations of physical anxiety—the breathing disorder, the muscles tightening, and the fingers tingling—coupled with the mental experience of anxiety.

I needed to work on developing the optimal experience, which is, actually, just being myself. Your optimal experience is your *you*—seeing yourself as an individual but also seeing that you're reflective of everyone else, and that everyone else is reflective of you.

STAYING IN THE PRESENT

In one of our first talks, Dr. Case took a notepad and drew a pendulum swinging back and forth.

She wanted me to see that one big reason we have anxiety

is that *we are not in the present*. If you're in the present state of mind, you're thinking about and noticing what is happening around you at that very moment. You're noticing how you feel. You can look around and think, *I'm okay at this very moment. The breeze is blowing through my hair. I see the sunlight glistening off the pond over there. I'm breathing well. I have plenty to eat. I'm not even thirsty.* In other words, presently, YOU'RE FINE!

The trick is *staying* in the present. It's so hard to stay in that frame of mind. I've learned anxiety comes when you have either guilt about the past or fear about the future.

Let me repeat that: you get anxious when you feel *guilt* about something in the past, or you *fantasize fearfully* about the future.

I've found that if you get the pendulum to stay still in the middle—in the present, in other words—you are less likely to have anxiety. And that's very difficult to do.

If you were to measure your thoughts for just five minutes, how many of them would actually fall in the present?

Here's what's happening in my brain right now in a short time.

- Wonder what we should have for dinner? (Future)
- Remember that time we baked the turkey in a plastic bag that melted right to it? (Past)
- My sister-in-law will probably insist on baking this year's Thanksgiving meal. I can see it now. She'll burn it in the convection oven again. (Future)
- Rocco, the dog, looks so tired right now from swimming in the lake! (Present)
- The manufacturing jobs in Ohio are going to dry up.

What will my brother do for a job? How will he pay for my niece's college? (Future)

- What if my niece doesn't continue her schooling? She won't be able to rely on finding a factory job. (Future)
- I can't believe my sister and I used to put sand in my brother's mouth when he was a toddler. (Past)
- It was her idea. (Past)
- Will Tim and I have long, healthy lives together? Wonder what we'll look like as geezers? (Future)
- I'm going to color my hair until I'm too feeble to be wheeled into the salon. I'm thinking what an eighty-year-old with long brunette hair will look like. (Future)
- Will we be happy when we're that old if we don't have kids now? (Future)
- I wish he'd stop watching football on TV while I'm trying to write this book. (Present)
- I was mistaken when I thought it was going to be easy to write this book. (Past)

See how hard and almost unnatural it is to stay in the present?

WHAT I'VE LEARNED: The present is where you are most aware of the things happening around you, and where you're most in tune with yourself. The present is where you can get creative and surprise yourself with the things you can do.

CONFIDENCE BOOSTER: Try to keep your mind on the

present, even for a short time, like ten minutes. Notice the colors around you. Notice how your body feels, how your back muscles feel. Be alert to your surroundings and see the things you notice in the present that would fly past you if you were daydreaming or fantasizing.

As a news operation we stress the stories that are happening *right now*. When you see BREAKING NEWS splashed across your television, what do you do? Most of us stop in our tracks and check it out, because "breaking" is supposed to mean it's important and happening *right now*!

If you read the paper, you generally find out what's already happened. You look at the sports schedule for the evening, and that's in the future. But when you hear me say, "Happening at this hour" you realize the news pendulum is in the middle, or on something currently transpiring.

Likewise, our brains are more "on" if we can get our personal thought pendulum to be more in the middle.

"I'm *on* today!" my husband will tell me when he feels he's firing on all cylinders at work. These are the days he is most "in the present," not fearing the future or feeling guilty about the speed bumps his business may have hit in the past. It is in these moments that he is able to pick up on the nuances of customers' voices—tuning in to their concerns or needs—even though they're calling from hundreds of miles away. He is able to accomplish so much more "in the present"! I gather it's a lot like what Dr. Wayne W. Dyer, in his book *The Power of Intention*, calls the "full vibrational spectrum."

The more you can stay in the present—and not imagine or feel fear about the future and not romanticize or feel guilt or embarrassment about the past—the more you're likely to realize: *Huh! I'm okay right now. Actually, I'm* good *right now! I'm all right.*

ROMANTICIZING THE PAST

Of course, I *did* have remorse and embarrassment—I was embarrassed that I had these panic episodes. And I kept reliving them. Before they finally quit coming with a vengeance, I estimate I had at least thirty of them.

Strangely enough, after they started I began romanticizing the past. Growing up in a small town in Ohio, I enjoyed a youth that revolved around cheerleading. My self-image was largely formed by the popularity that brought me.

During the time of my first anxiety attacks, I started thinking about my old cheerleading uniforms from junior high, high school, and some of college. By that time I was twenty-nine or thirty years old, mind you! But I remembered how soft some of them were, especially the ones for indoor basketball. (The ones for football were itchy and woolen.) And I thought about how the used uniforms passed down from the older squads rarely fit me, and how I'd diet the week before we were measured for new skirts because I wanted the smallest size. (Who knows why?)

I hadn't thought about that in years, but there I was obsessing: *Oh, it would be so much fun to have one of these pleated skirts we used to wear!* So off I went to that global yard sale, eBay. And you're darn right they had cheerleading uniforms! Authentic ones. Retro ones. Vintage ones. Red ones. Blue ones. Costume ones. Skanky ones. Name your color and size, and you could find it there.

I kept finding myself going online to look at them. Then I'd think, *I might use this for Halloween, but other than that, why in heck do I want this?* This was a clear-cut example of romanticizing the past, Dr. Case said. "Life was so simple then," she explained. "You didn't deal with anxiety, not on this level, anyway." And she said, "You're buying something that reminds you of that, because you physically want to be back there."

I thought that was brilliant, though it was so obvious I should have seen it myself. Nostalgia is a huge thing in our culture, whether it's in music or in decor.

FEARING THE FUTURE AND FANTASIZING ABOUT IT

Now, in terms of why my pendulum would swing to the future, bringing up fear or imagined fantasy, well, that was easy, too. I fantasized about all the terrible things that could go wrong in my job, in my life, or in my house.

The moment I had my first anxiety attack, I had fleeting thoughts about the (near) future:

- What if I can't make it to the sound bite?
- If I lose my breath, my bosses will see it, and I'll get into trouble.
- I could lose my job over this.
- I could lose my house over this.

And on it went, until I had scared myself right into what felt like a heart attack! I was fantasizing about what *could* happen (mess-up) instead of what was indeed happening at that very moment. (The news show was starting. Big deal!)

Most of us fear the unknown on some level. The way to counteract that fear, in our minds, is to plan, plan, plan. Let's be clear: planning and preparing are good. But while we are prudently preparing for the future, most of us also tend to make up little movies and stories that trip us up, because in our minds the unknown is precisely that—unknown. The longer we stay in fantasyland, the more it allows our pendulums to swing to the future.

If I can make that pendulum be still, I can stay in the present. And if I can stay in the present, I can quiet my anxiety.

AN ATTITUDE OF GRATITUDE

Get this: the single easiest way to stay in the present is to think about the things around you for which you are grateful. Gratitude is a fantastic tool, because it forces you to notice what you have now—not what hurt you before, not what you're afraid of in the future, but what you are *now*. No matter what anybody else thinks of you. It's a great way to assess all the things you should be confident about concerning yourself!

So right now:

- Aren't you grateful for the eyes with which you can read? Be grateful you *can* read.

- In this moment, I'm saying "Thank you" for the air-conditioning blowing up through the kitchen chairs as I write this.
- And I'm grateful for being up past my bedtime, because I have tomorrow off.
- I'm grateful that I can type pretty fast to keep up with my thoughts while I write this book for you to read.

See, being grateful forces you to think about where you are and what you have this very second. If you're thinking about reading this book *now*, you are in the present. Bravo!

DALE CARNEGIE, GOD OF POPULARITY

In my first talk with Dr. Case, I mentioned that in the summer before I started eighth grade, I saw a publication on my father's nightstand that I could not ignore. It was the grandfather of how-to and self-help books: Dale Carnegie's *How to Win Friends and Influence People.*

How to win friends! Gasp. My eyes flew open in anticipation at the thought. *Thank you, O merciful God of training bras and junior high dances! I'm gonna influence people to like me!*

Okay, not a very noble cause for this great info. But when you're an eighth-grade girl in the throes of puberty and subject to the mercy of smart-alecky boys ("Deformed" was the nickname one boy gave me, describing my string-bean figure back then), this book seemed like a godsend. It may as well have been made in the shape of a homecoming queen crown.

I had such concrete plans for whatever pieces of sage advice lay inside this beacon of truth! No, I didn't see it as an unassuming paperback adorning my parents' bedstand. To me it looked like the Holy Grail of junior high popularity.

You may have guessed my dad had been reading it because as a preacher he wanted to know the best way to get out his message. I can still recall picking it up and reading the back cover. It said that Carnegie's technique had been changing lives since the book was first published in 1937.

Fwwwwwwp fwwwwp fwwwp.

I flipped so fast through the pages you'd have thought they were the wrapping for the chocolate bar holding the golden ticket to Willy Wonka's chocolate factory. After finding the table of contents I headed straight for the section that mattered to me: "Six Ways to Make People Like You." Bingo! And I must have stood there for an hour, not flinching, reading the summary tips and the corresponding chapters, including:

Principle 1
Become genuinely interested in other people.
Principle 3
Remember that a person's name is to that person the sweetest and most important sound in any language.
Principle 4
Be a good listener. Encourage others to talk about themselves.

Holy jamoly! my eighth-grade self said. *This is so easy! Why haven't I thought of these ideas before?*

It was no-nonsense. Internalizing this info so early in life was key in my development. Even at that young age, and already getting attention for my activities at school (cheerleading, choir, band), I was cognizant of wanting to be more popular and in the big picture, graduating to bigger stages and bigger audiences.

So I read that book, and read it, and read it.

Those Dale Carnegie tips were revolutionary to someone that young. I took notes and employed the tips, and you know what? They worked! Hot diggety!

I wanted to be more influential, and I was. And I became a leader, a class officer, and well liked.

I continued to follow the Carnegie advice all the way through high school. I think those how-to's—along with guidance from my parents to always make other people feel good and important and let them know you genuinely care about them—helped me win homecoming queen years later. It's as if that little paperback helped shape who I became!

WE ALL WANT TO BE LIKED

The funny thing is that those tips really play to my job right now. People are kind enough to figuratively invite me into their homes when they decide they'll watch our show. You're not going to invite someone into your home if you don't like him or her. (I watch people I think I would like in real life.) Therefore, I need to be likable on camera.

And it certainly helps to be approachable when you go out in the field as a reporter and ask total strangers to open up to you. My personal interviewing style isn't aggressive or in-your-face. My m.o. is to make someone feel comfortable so he'll *want* to open up to me.

So how do I do that? I get interested in the person. As far as the *influencing* part of Carnegie's title, in my profession it's not that journalists especially want to influence people—in fact, we are to be impartial. But I think it's fair to say that the current events we decide to put in our show influence what you'll be thinking and chatting about that day. (Watercooler, 9 a.m.: Hey, Marge! Did you see that story about 17 percent of people saying they'd take their BlackBerry over their spouse if they had to choose? I'd chuck 'em both if I could! Bwaaa haaa!)

NOBODY LIKES ME, EVERYBODY HATES ME

I told Dr. Case that the desire to be liked was always a driving force in my life. I want to be held in high esteem, and I want people to honestly say, "I like you." I've thought about it for as long as I can remember.

There's a family story that I'll share with you. I'm the middle child, between sister Tonda (three years older) and brother Kevin (two years younger). I don't remember what precipitated the behavior I'm about to describe. Try to stifle your giggles here as you read it:

When I was a toddler—well before I started school—I would sit on the stairs at our house and just boo-hoo. I'd work myself into a frenzy and cry, "Nobody loves me, everybody hates me!" Tonda says that about the third or fourth time I pulled this, it evolved from a crying session into my *singing* about how nobody loved me. (Did I have early aspirations for Broadway or somethin'?) I certainly put myself center stage, like, "Let's just enjoy this while I'm at it!"

Now, my sister still laughs about how she and Mom would sit on the living room couch for my "show." They could see only my chubby toddler legs perched on the top stair steps, where I'd sit and boo-hoo. Their view of just the knees down made it more comical. And by the time I got to the singing part, they'd practically convulse with laughter. Tonda still says, "You were such a little drama queen!"

I have no idea why I convinced myself everybody hated me. Tonda thinks it happened when somebody denied me something, or told me no, which would just break my heart. But I remember that it felt real to my little self. Maybe it was just middle-child syndrome. My brother had some medical problems—the ball joints of his hips deteriorated and had to be replaced when he was quite young—and my sister was very vocal. So maybe this was my way of saying, "Notice me!"

I still don't want to be overlooked. Who does? But I think I might have carried this a little further than most people. I told Dr. Case that as far back as school, anger and hurt fueled my desire to be accepted on a grander scale, and I tried to work on myself or on whoever I thought had rejected me. I was very serious about it. I'd sit and stew over it, asking, *What is wrong with me?*

That wasn't the best way to go about it, of course, but I was a teenager, and you learn such things only through the wisdom of growing up. Eventually I came to a different realization.

WHAT I'VE LEARNED: Whenever you learn someone disdains you, instead of looking at yourself and asking, *What's wrong with me?*, ask yourself, *What kind of energy do I give off that doesn't agree with that other person's energy?*

CONFIDENCE BOOSTER: Thinking from the other person's point of view helps you avoid labeling yourself or the other person as "wrong" or "bad." Think of your conflict in terms of energy. Try to figure out where the other person's negative or positive train of thought is originating from. Consider that person's fears, concerns, and point of view. Then consider your own. It may not alleviate the conflict or dislike between you, but it will certainly be healthier for you to recognize that the two of you clash for reasons other than whether you're "likable" or not. Give it a try!

The Takeaway

You can think only one thought at one time. Try to do otherwise. You'll notice your thoughts come in an order of succession. If you are thinking thoughts of gratitude, you are in the present. If you are in the present, you are not fantasizing about the future or feeling guilty about the past. You just *are*. And you are confident about what you currently are: being, breathing, living. In the present.

Robin's Ramblings

If you can't lose it, decorate it.

(*Note:* I saw this in a book called *Don't Blame Me, Sister!* by greeting card company MikWright. Turns out that saying is also the title of a book by Anita Renfroe. I use it as a response when people compliment my outfit. It's a funny statement about our body image issues and attire.)

6

WHAT'S ON YOUR PEDESTAL?

The Difference Between Being Liked and Being Respected

When I first told Dr. Case that I'd read the Carnegie book and implemented it in my everyday life, I wasn't prepared for her reaction.

She laughed.

And then she said, "What's the result?"

"Well, I make friends with everyone."

"But what's the result?" she pressed.

I thought the answer was obvious, but I played along, not sure where this was going. "People like me," I said.

"Who doesn't like you?" she asked.

I couldn't think of anyone, so I said, "No one."

"What?"

"Yes. Everyone generally likes me."

"Robin, you mean to tell me when you're smiling on TV and then have to tell your audience that someone was stabbed to death, they like you? If I saw you, I'd say, 'Shut your trap!'"

She might as well have slapped me. I was totally taken

aback. I wasn't sure what to say. I just muttered, "Oh, Dr. Case, you're kidding."

But she wasn't. "Look," she said, "when I first met you, you grabbed both of my hands, you gave me that kooky double handshake with a smile and a soft voice, and I thought, 'What a phony baloney!'"

I'm sure I looked shocked. No one had ever said anything like this to me. My double-handed handshake was my secret tool for making people feel warm and welcome in my home! My mind trailed off into what other devices I could use to make people feel important when I met them.

"Robin," she quickly added, "I didn't say I didn't like you. I just said, 'What a phony baloney.' But you're missing something. Not everything about you is likable. If you're not a bitch to your coworkers, for sure you're a bitch to Tim."

I just sat with my mouth hanging open. Gaper's delay, I call it.

Dr. Case was trying to get me to realize an exceedingly important point: *we all have moments when we are unlikable.* And we must embrace and love all the things about ourselves that we don't like and keep locked away in compartments, if we are to truly accept ourselves and others.

But back to the part where she proclaimed I was a bitch. *Huh?* Well, okay, I do have freak-outs every now and then, if just to make a point to Tim at home. ("You *never* hear what I'm saying, you daydreaming space cadet!")

Dr. Case made me see that I was putting other people's opinions of me on a pedestal. Or, in my case, I was putting the viewer up on a pedestal. I was putting *you* on a pedestal. (Of course you deserve to be there, doll!)

Let me get serious here: because I held other people's views of me in such high esteem, by relation I put *myself* lower than them. And that's where the panic arose. Without realizing it, I was infatuated with the audience's opinions of me.

Because I was putting the viewing public up on a pedestal, I was willing to not be liked by my husband, even if I realized I was bitchy or nasty in my demands to him, in attempts to quell my panic attacks.

Part of the work Dr. Case and I had to do was to knock down the importance of other people's opinions of me (in my mind at least) and bring up my own opinion of my entire self. In other words, to restore my self-confidence.

What this really meant was I had to learn *how to be confrontational* and assertive, if in a nice way! Now, I hate confrontation. When I thought of confronting someone and his thinking badly of me, my heart beat so fast. It was absolutely fight-or-flight, and honey, this bird was flying, not fighting! So I had to learn to embrace both sides of my personality—the confrontational, not-so-likable part of me, as well as the part that I was happy to show the rest of the world.

In other words, I had to embrace my inner bitch!

WHO YOU CALLIN' A BITCH?

To embrace my inner bitch, I had to let go of my vision of myself as a goody two-shoes, because I was denying the other part of my personality. It wasn't realistic. You know, there are days when we're going to be angels, and then there are days that we're just hell on wheels. And I wasn't being authentic with myself if I didn't allow that part of me to surface, recognize it, and love it.

Granted, that doesn't mean you should ride in on a broom and zap your nosy neighbor with a lightning bolt. Dr. Case and I worked on this steadily, and it took me a while to get it. I kept thinking of my sister. One of the most admirable traits about her, in my opinion, is her honesty. I've always said, if you want to know how you look, go ask Tonda. ("How do you look? Bloated, that's how you look," she would answer, if that were the case.) Now, it's not exactly enjoyable all the time, because *she will tell you the truth*. While I'm of the belief there are ways to be diplomatic without hurting someone's feelings, she goes for the blunt approach. I respect that! She is honest without fear of what people will think of her.

Dr. Case and I embarked on an "Embrace Your Inner Bitch" campaign for a while. She would say, "C'mon, what did you really want to say today? Don't even repress it. What's the benefit of your being a goody-goody here? Don't you see there are drawbacks to constantly pleasing other people? As long as you put others on a pedestal, they'll control you, and you will never rise above them and expand your own sphere of influence."

Wow! That's deep. More on that attractive concept, expanding your own sphere of influence, later. Meanwhile, keep reading.

RESPECT = HALF CORRECTION, HALF ADMIRATION

I was certain that what I wanted more than anything was to be admired. But Dr. Case helped me see that being respected is so much better. And to ascend to the level of respect, I was going to have to learn to confront people. Respect, she says, equals half correction, half admiration.

Let's talk about that equation. Haven't there been times when you didn't have the backbone to tell someone the truth, especially if it involved any negativity? In work situations years ago I'd opt to give people just positive feedback instead of calling them on the carpet, even when I knew they hadn't given their best effort and had affected our quality on air. As a result I may have earned their favor temporarily, but I wasn't earning their respect, because deep down they knew I didn't have the guts to give them the constructive criticism (or correction) their performance deserved. And, to be honest, I wasn't respecting myself because I didn't feel the confidence to tell them what I was really feeling.

For example: say I have a new producer whose work is still subpar months after he's been hired. I would feel more comfortable smiling and telling him he's doing just fine, instead of getting into the uncomfortable business of telling him he isn't producing the caliber of show that our audience expects and we require.

In that split second after I told him, "Good job!" and gave him the office equivalent of a coach smacking a player on the butt, he might like me. But I wouldn't be earning his respect unless I told him the truth—that he needed to improve (correction).

Just today we had a new producer doing the seven o'clock show. She was just having a hell of a time: video was lost. Stories didn't show up. Then we had a two-minute taped report fall into a black hole somewhere and were left scrambling to fill it with viable stories. (Two minutes is eons in television news.) In addition to mishaps beyond her control, she put her show together in a sterile, unfeeling way, not taking into account what the viewers truly care about.

I could have just said, "Tomorrow's a new day. Drink some NyQuil and let's start with a clean slate tomorrow!" Instead, in the interest of our viewers, I told her what she did well, then talked honestly about what I would have liked to have seen in the show, and why.

It wasn't the most comfortable of situations, but I *gained* her respect by being honest with her. And I *gave* her respect by not taking the easy route. In the long run, it made me feel more confident about my abilities to be assertive, while helping develop her abilities as a producer.

Here's another example of half correction, half admiration, using what's called "the insult sandwich" around our office.

The admiration:

Boss says: "Good ratings this week! You guys are on a roll!"

The correction:

Boss squeezes his brow. "You've got to pare down that podcast. It's using too many of our editing hours. We're having to use two editors instead of one, doubling the cost of this online ditty."

The admiration:

Boss returns to pleasantries. "But you guys constantly get five-star ratings on the podcast on iTunes! Great!"

So in this fictitious example, he spoke his mind and gave constructive criticism while not alienating me, his employee.

Being respected is more important in developing your confidence than just being liked is. If you've earned someone's respect, you've accomplished more than just having him or her "like" you.

EVERY NOW AND THEN, HIT THE RESET BUTTON

I have a dear friend whom I can count on to give me a pat Pollyanna answer when I ask her how she's doing.

"I'm fine! Blessed! Great!" she'll reply. She's always fine. Even when I know she's not, she will usually deny herself the release of saying "This ticked me off today!" or "Geez, I wish my husband would help with the kids more!" It's like the wannabe actresses you see in Hollywood at the sidewalk cafés, smiling and posing in case there's a movie director around.

For her own benefit, I want to shake her and say, "Sometimes you've gotta get real with your feelings! You don't always have to be 'on,' girlfriend!"

Now, when people are around, unless it's your spouse or maybe your closest friend, most of us *are* on to some degree. I'm even on when my parents are around, because I don't want them to worry. I know what makes them comfortable and happy, therefore I'm on. And even when I'm having a conversation with a friend, we're still feeding off of each other's energy, whether we're exchanging ideas or feeling each other's mood that day. You affect every person you come into contact with in a positive or negative way.

It's almost like the engine of the boat Tim and I use at the lake. When the key is off, everything's at zero. When the key is on, the RPMs register. And RPMs directly affect the oil pressure. Oil pressure directly affects the water temperature. You get a whole chain of effects from this energy that flows. And when you turn the key off, it all goes back to zero.

I've come to believe that to be off—to find your authentic self—you really need to go back to zero as much as possible. Some people do it through meditation. Others do it through prayer. Still someone else might do it by playing with her dog. No matter how you do it, it's extremely important to get it done. In our society it's very difficult to center ourselves, because we're taught to *be* on, to be busy doing something, accomplishing.

I once had a coanchor named Charles who saw how tired I was all the time, and how driven I was to accomplish things. One day he said, "Sleep *is* an accomplishment." He's right! And likewise, getting back to zero, or centering yourself, is an accomplishment.

I find I can center myself at a lake where my husband and I have a little weekender cottage. Did you ever look out your window and see a sunset that just brought tears to your eyes? That's how I feel at the lake. It's laid back and nobody's froufrou. We spend a whole lot of the time doing nothing at that cottage, when we actually find the time to get there!

The lake area is wonderfully conducive to rest, and that's what I need when I go there. I call it the No Makeup Zone, because I'm not News Superwoman out there. It's where I can act a little stupid and sit around in my pajamas and flip-flops. Matter of fact, today I'm writing this section of the book at the lake house. It's 2 p.m., and I'm wearing a pajama shirt with golfing shorts. Pretty.

WHAT I'VE LEARNED: Don't be afraid to ask for help to get your mind back to "zero." I know most people don't have the time or chance to head to a lake to relax. But even if you're an exhausted mother with a baby and a near-empty bank account, you still need to find a way to give yourself some downtime. Find a sitter one night a month whom you can pay by bartering a service you can provide for her. Go to a friend's house for an afternoon playdate with your kids. Does your church have a day care where you can take the children on Saturday for a couple of hours so you can spend quality time with your husband? If not, a trusted family member or friend will surely come to your aid.

CONFIDENCE BOOSTER: If you can't physically get away from it all, see if you can meditate or reset your mind a few times a week. It could help you stay connected to your authentic self.

INFATUATION VS. RESENTMENT

It doesn't matter who you are, or your level of power, money, or intellect. People get into the same patterns. They may get infatuated with something or become resentful about something. And they allow it to completely control their conscious experience. Then that manifests in...well, it's almost like a measure of physics. You can't have a one-sided magnet. Where there's one experience, you're going to have the other.

The harder I tried to repress these parts of myself—my true

self—the more I'd actually attract the events that would put them right in my face. That's what made me panic.

In retrospect, I see the timing of it all was quite interesting. One of the carrots Dr. Case dangles with someone who's ambitious—and I've already admitted I set my goals high—is that sphere of influence I mentioned earlier. Dr. Case will normally say to people, "Look, you have a certain level of influence, and you can expand that sphere, but you need a new strategy. What you're doing now is not going to work. Look around you. You have no new opportunities."

When I began working with Dr. Case, I told her I wanted to be on national television. The more I thought about working at the network level, the more I grew infatuated with the whole thing, and the more I wanted to hide the parts of myself I thought would keep me from actually getting there.

WHAT I'VE LEARNED: If there's a part of yourself that you disown, that piece of yourself that you repress or suppress will keep recycling itself to be your primary object of work. Your inner self will try to show you over and over again what aspects you need to embrace so that you can have the opportunity to love yourself.

CONFIDENCE BOOSTER: Understand that this is about the divinity of life. You can't even *do* any other work except the work on your psyche if you refuse to love a whole category of yourself. If you can grasp this concept, you're moving closer to accepting yourself.

From the beginning, Dr. Case kept pounding into me that I completely refused to acknowledge the part of myself that was bitchy and nasty. The fact that I kept seeing myself as a Pollyanna, always happy, always likable, was drowning me. I was the last person on earth to see that in some ways I was still that little girl, sitting at the top of the stairs crying that nobody loved her.

WHAT I'VE LEARNED: Respect is higher on the ladder of confidence than just being liked. Think about it...you feel confident when someone likes you. But you throw out the infatuation with being liked when you decide to be respected. It's one rung up that ladder.

CONFIDENCE BOOSTER: Recognize where you've evolved up the ladder of confidence by choosing to gain someone's respect instead of just their admiration.

The Takeaway

If you have a problem with anxiety, I urge you to talk with someone about it. Not only will you be helping yourself, but you'll also help remove the stigma associated with such emotional distress. A lot of people might see me on TV and think, *She's got it easy. She's got no problems! What a fairy-tale life!*

The reality is that every job, including mine and yours, paid or not, presents challenges. Thank goodness I am surrounded by incredibly talented people—from the writers, producers, and directors to the makeup people. (Have you seen this face before the glam squad gets a hold of me? Honey!)

The point I'm trying to make is that it's dangerous for young people to assume someone else's accomplishments came easily. It's important to tell your story about fear, self-doubt, or self-criticism, and embark on a journey of learning to find yourself worthy. The problem won't go away on its own. It's an ever-present issue. Learn to stay fixed on finding your way out, and tell yourself, *Whatever the block is, I'm going to surmount it.* Be open to a path.

Robin's Ramblings

It's good to be wanted. (Remember this saying when it feels as if everybody and his brother is pulling at your pant leg wanting you to do something for him. When everyone wants a piece of you, change your attitude about it and remember—it's good to be wanted.

7

STOP JUDGING YOURSELF!

Is This the Secret to Confidence?

Have you ever felt as if you were your own worst enemy? None of us ever means to be. But in resisting *being* myself at first and in carrying such strict judgments of my actions, that's exactly what I was: my own worst enemy.

Dr. Case kept trying to tell me that once I started loving myself and found myself worthy of love even for my dark side, the anxiety would go away. Absolutely. Just like, "Poof!" Gone. Sounds like such an easy prescription. I thought, *Yeah, easy for you to say, lady. How do I do that?*

I was starting to see that the Pollyanna side I prided myself on was severely limiting my possibilities. When I started finding out I was lovable and worthy of love—even when I was cranky, piling on the pounds, or calling someone a pinhead under my breath—the more I appreciated that those things have benefits for myself *and other people*. They weren't all drawbacks! That's not to say all of them would be pleasant, but when I could see that it wasn't just a lopsided experience, like, *Oh, when I'm out of sorts it hurts everyone,* I was making progress.

I see now that I had incredibly black-and-white perceptions and limiting views. In my mind, I was a success or I was a failure. Then I would focus on what I thought were failures. I was good or bad. I was this or that. Dr. Case worked with me to formulate strategies to get past those limiting ideas.

But when I'd take a step forward, I'd think it was a permanent step. Dr. Case said, "When you expand your love, it doesn't mean you're done. You're never free of responsibility. You'll just keep expanding your sphere of influence. So the next time you get stuck, you'll be just as stuck as you were this time, because it's in familiar territory."

This is really high-minded thinking here. Stay with me. If you're having a hard time understanding what she means by "your sphere of influence," try this:

She says that when people feel that they have the "aha" moment, the dangerous side of that is the cockiness, the feeling that you're not going to have that problem you've overcome anymore. The truth of that, she says, is that you have more power because you found out something about yourself. But the responsibility of that power is that areas of your life expand. And the result is that you'll have more opportunity at work, more opportunity financially. But when you expand through life, it is more responsibility. It's more to think about. It's more to manage. It's more decisions to make. In other words, the moment you think you've just overcome your challenge…*at that exact moment* you have attracted a whole new set of challenges, she says. This is what she means by "expanding your sphere of influence."

But if you disown any part of yourself, you become stuck in the sphere. The silver lining is that at least by then I was developing techniques for getting *un*stuck.

YOU ARE WORTHY!

In my experience the Demartini Method became a way of finding myself worthy. It simply asks questions. The answers put certain information into the nervous system to override the present labels. They force you to work through your thoughts. Basically, you think your way out of whatever your hang-up is (for me, anxiety)!

(Disclaimer: Please note that as a journalist I have to be objective and fair. However, in this book I'm telling you my experience, so it will be presented as such—my experience. I recognize that it may be subjective, but this is not a direct endorsement or a promise that this method will work for everyone, nor should it be construed as such. Okay, I'll put down the blackboard pointer now and shoo the lawyers off my back. Ha!)

Based on a set of twenty-one organized questions, the Demartini Method explores the universal laws and principles of human existence. They're designed to give dimension to your experience. Now, they're beautiful questions, but they're just questions. Some people have said to Dr. Case, "Oh, the Method is so intellectual. What does it have to do with the heart?" And to be fair, she says, intellect does sometimes get in the way of the heart with really bright individuals.

(Did she think I was bright? Cool! Oops, there I go again, putting other people's opinions up on a pedestal.)

The key is the nuance with which people follow through with

the answers. The questions are very methodical, and they've been tried with literally hundreds of thousands of people.

As I've said, the premise is about pushing through the barriers that hold us back from experiencing our true natures. In a sense, the Method is a manual for understanding why we make the decisions we do in our lives, and for re-creating ourselves in ways to fulfill our purpose for being here.

(Dang, let me put down my diet pop. This is *deep*!)

START WITH ONE WORD

In working with a client, the first thing Dr. Case—or any facilitator—does is establish an opinion, using some sort of word that reflects the belief of the client. This can either be a good or a bad description of the person, event, or thing.

For example, after a discussion about the people in a person's life—say that evil coworker who just drives the client nuts—the ensuing conversation might go like this:

Client: "George is *mean*."

Facilitator: "Who sees *you* as being mean to the same degree and magnitude that you see George being mean?"

The preconceived notion is that being mean is bad. So George is bad. The facilitator tells the client to answer that question to help find the balance:

Client: Nobody. I'm not as mean as George.

Facilitator: Well, let's think about who sees you as mean. Who saw you as mean when you were young? Who thinks you're mean now?

The facilitator continues to ask questions until the client realizes…

Client: Oh, my God, I've been as mean as George! I cannot even believe it! Yeah, I'm mean, too! Maybe in a different way to different people, but I'm just as mean. Being mean is bad.

Facilitator: What are the *benefits* of that bad thing? In other words, what are the benefits of George being mean to you?

Client: Nothing! There are no benefits to his being mean. It sucks!

It may seem as if this is just going around in circles. But this is where you have to pay close attention. The facilitator then has to push the client and ask, "What are the benefits to *others* of your having been mean to them?" (I'll explain more about the benefits of these "bad things" in the pages ahead.) The wording of the question gets rid of the feeling of guilt or judgment that being mean is purely bad. The facilitator might go through seven or ten characteristics, such as *mean*, *selfish*, *irresponsible*, or *nasty*. It might take three or four hours to get through five or ten topics. It's really work! The process is simple but complex at the same time. The questions are a science, but the process is an art.

In a sense, it's really just sitting there listening to your facilitator and yourself and concentrating intently. Of course, the facilitator has to be experienced at finding out what the client is trying to escape—what topics make her squirm. And the facilitator also has to have a wide database of benefits, in case clients think there are only drawbacks to certain characteristics.

TELLING ON MYSELF

On certain things, man, I would be so stubborn! I just wouldn't want to see the other side. We *both* had to have great staying power. Believe me, sometimes the hours we worked together were excruciating!

For example, Dr. Case asked me to see how the panic attacks served me. I thought, *How do they "serve" me? What do you mean, "serve" me?* I just looked at her as if she had two heads. It so completely confounded me that I couldn't see any way in the world those damn things *helped* me!

"I don't think I get it," I said. "The body should not have panic attacks. It means the person's weak. I have panic attacks, they're bad, and they're going to ruin me on the air, so I have to hide them."

"Robin," Dr. Case reminded me, "you're looking at them in a very fixed way, as bad. *Bad* is a label. Let's try it again. Okay, what's the benefit? What are the *great* things about having panic attacks?"

I was flummoxed.

Dr. Case explained that if I could do this complete turnaround—learn *not* to think they were bad—they wouldn't come again. If I thought, *This doesn't feel good, but it's going to serve me,* then I wouldn't fear them and they wouldn't materialize.

She challenged me: "Find twenty-five to forty benefits of your panic attacks. How did they create trouble for others?

How did they benefit you? Think of this in the present, past, and future. Write down the disadvantages in all areas of life—financial, physical, mental, spiritual, vocational, social, and familial. Then, how does that serve others?"

"Well," I said, "they serve me in that I've started eating better," since I wondered if it was all the sugar and caffeine I ingested that made me leap into the feeling of heart failure. Then I added, "I've started paying attention and eating more protein."

I continued, "I got into bounce-a-quarter-off-your-butt shape because I would exercise before the show to try to wear myself out and stabilize my heart rate."

Here's one of the biggies:

"It makes me grateful that Tim supports and loves me regardless of this problem."

Early on in my therapy, of course, I still had recurring panic attacks on the air, and I really, *really* dreaded them. Interestingly, I never had them anywhere else. Why? Because that was my fear. I was the breadwinner. I was going to screw it up. I had a good job and what if, what if, what if—right? I was so wrapped up in my title and my position that I constantly fantasized about the future and the bad outcome of my panic attacks. So I thought, *Maybe I am taking better care of myself now, but these panic attacks are still a disservice to me because they interrupt my train of thought on the job.*

Then I had to turn that around and think, *How is* that *good?* That took a little bit of flexibility, but I decided, *That disservice is good in that it makes me question whether I'm on purpose in my life.*

Get it? I had to go back and forth until I didn't *fear* them anymore. Instead of trying to calm myself by saying, "I'm okay right now," I had to *empower* myself. I had to think, *Thank you, God, may I have another?* You know, *Bring it on!* Then I could think of them as "purpose attacks" and give them a positive connotation. Seeing them as "purpose attacks" instead of "anxiety attacks" made me *grateful* for them. That way, they'd help me get back to my purpose in life and realize how I felt about myself.

Whoa! I'm talking *progress* here!

REPEAT, REPEAT THIS PROCESS

So we did this over and over, because I had groups of things I'd given cut-and-dried labels like "It's better to be liked than disliked." She kept taking me back to that one, because she felt that was the underlying cause of my anxiety and loss of confidence. And I obviously had more work to do there, because I still really couldn't stand the idea that anyone would dislike me. I'd worked so hard at being liked all my life.

In a very serious tone, Dr. Case told me this limiting belief would sink me, because it would control me. *Rather than my being in control of myself, the belief was controlling me.* So she challenged: "Robin, tell me where it's as fantastic to be disliked as it is to be liked. Give me as many benefits and reasons as you can for being disliked."

This went against everything I had trained myself to believe, so I had to do a lot of mental gymnastics. Once I did, some of the benefits really surprised me.

For example, when you think about it, if you're disliked, you actually get some downtime to work on your own *self*, or use it to be with your hubby, or your best bud, or just chill out! If people don't like you, fewer of them will be clamoring to be with you! C'mon, where is the time in the day for just chillin' out? Cool! Hey, it may sound silly, but there's truth to this!

And once I started firing on those cylinders, I found a gazillion reasons to be disliked! And things started to click. Finally I was able to say, "Hey, it's totally worth being disliked!" And once I started seeing things from this perspective, I started to have fun. Dr. Case said she could see a real change in me. *I was starting to crack the door on a breakthrough.*

BREAKTHROUGH? GEE, DON'T MIND IF I DO!

Here's the supposed science of it: the more you build up information in the nervous system that we call the mind, the more it balances out previously registered information. Dr. Case explains it this way: "When thoughts keep going back-forth, back-forth, back-forth, all of a sudden, *zip!* Right in the middle, they create a spark of *optimal experience.*"

In other words:

When this happens with human thoughts, people often don't even know why. But they know they're experiencing something meaningful on the highest level, and it's all-encompassing. They become silent, they're humbled, they get tears of gratitude and love in their eyes, and suddenly things seem to make sense. And they feel connected to their own higher source and power, which is really where they gain their answers.

I theorized it must feel a lot like those Sunday mornings in the church pews: that moment of gratitude and feeling of connection with the Creator when you're sitting in prayer meditating on what really matters. That feeling of acceptance, and of accepting everyone and everything else.

The theory is, the more someone practices seeing both sides of everything, the closer he gets to the point of optimal experience. And people around him can't help but be moved by it! They *feel* that. It's like the attraction of a moth to a light. People want to be near that person or associate with him in one way or another. It sounds like an extraordinary thing, doesn't it?

But before getting to that point—to that breakthrough—almost everybody wants to just give up, Dr. Case says. I understand why! There were days I'd say, "This feels like too much work!" My mind just fought it, and sometimes I developed a bombed-out sort of indifference. People will fight, fight, fight to keep the beliefs they've held for years—even if the beliefs are limiting or damaging.

DO THE HOMEWORK

I had to work on all the benefits of anxiety for three hours—with three separate pages for each category of life: financial, physical, mental, spiritual, vocational, social, and familial. Man! Dr. Case had me do a lot of writing, because if you write, you're taking action, and your brain responds to it better than if you just think something. Dr. Case held me to it, too, so she could find out where my conscious and subconscious were going.

Eventually I started letting go of whatever restrictions I originally had. But at first the hardest thing for me to let go of was the homework itself! Dr. Case would say, "Okay, show me your papers," and I'd go, "Uh, I don't think I want to give them over." I'd get all self-conscious and hold on to them for dear life. And Dr. Case would tease me. She'd say, "C'mon, give 'em over!" And we'd both laugh, and then finally I'd hand them to her.

It wasn't that I was afraid she would show them to somebody. I was over that by then, because I knew she was completely and totally confidential with her clients. I just didn't want her to have proof of what was going on in my brain! I was afraid of what would be written on those papers when she gave them back to me!

More on this in the next chapter.

WHAT I'VE LEARNED: Writing helps your brain feel as though you are taking action. It is much more therapeutic than just sitting there thinking and stewing.

CONFIDENCE BOOSTER: If you're trying to work through an issue, write about it! For example: you might fear you're about to get laid off at work. Indeed, what a difficult and trying thing! Write down the drawbacks of being laid off. That part should be easy, right? Then turn around and write down the *benefits* of getting laid off. That's a toughie. (One benefit could be that losing your job might kick you onto the vocational path you always wanted to be on, but needed more education for. This could be the catalyst to put you back in touch with your original "dream job.") Write in terms of the present, past, and future, and in the different areas of life: financial, physical, mental, spiritual, vocational, social, and familial. Nobody is saying this will be easy. While it will be uncomfortable, it will challenge your brain to do mental flips and as a result you may be more prepared should job cuts come your way. (Fingers crossed that they won't, however.)

The Takeaway

Do you need to get more balanced in your thoughts about yourself? If you can begin to see how there is good in the bad and bad in the good, you're on your way to balancing your thoughts in general. Think about it: even the greatest things in life come with pitfalls. Winning the lottery—great, right? Well, think of all the lottery winners who have gone on to waste their fortunes and wind up with nothing. Think how unsure they may feel about which people are really their friends, and which are just hanging around for a handout. Think about all the work they have to do with their accountants and the responsibilities of keeping up with all that money. Winning the lottery is good and bad.

The trick is to apply this thinking to yourself so that you can be balanced in your feelings about yourself. You are not good or bad. So if good and bad exist in the same things, don't you embody both? Deep thoughts, I know. For a second I felt as if I were back in the freshman philosophy class.

But here's the deal: to truly feel a deep confidence, I had to learn a) how to love myself, and b) how to find balance in my thoughts, in order to find balance in my life.

Robin's Ramblings

"Change is birthed in pain and opportunity."

—*Dr. Amelia Case*

Baby Robin. From about this age until the time I was five, I was regularly in the hospital for pneumonia, after surviving my premature birth. The curly hair would give my mom fits. She'd have Dad cut the knots out.

Elementary school–aged Robin. Here I am with my brother, Kevin, with whom I share a birthday, two years apart. About this time singing was something I figured everyone could do. I volunteered for solos in music class, and stood out on the lawn singing "The Star-Spangled Banner."

Sunday morning at the Meade house. I'm standing with my sister, Tonda. Don't you dig the granny dress and hat? My mother made sure we were dressed to the nines for church. I usually arrived at church with red puffy eyes because for some reason I could never find my shoes, and ended up crying about it. My sister's job was to find a matching pair of shoes for me every Sunday.

The Meade family during the teen years. Dad, Mom, Tonda, Kevin, and me. I'm wearing the Madonna-style lace in my hair and an outfit my mom sewed for me.

I firmly believe the information I learned in Dale Carnegie's *How to Win Friends and Influence People* led me to this moment: being crowned homecoming queen of New London High School in the fall of 1986. Classmate Ross Tolliver was king.

Standing with Julie during our college years. Even though I loved her sense of style as she pursued her education in fashion design, I thought she should be wearing a red cape as Superwoman! Our friendship is just as close to this day.

Big dreams, big hair. This is my sophomore year of college in Canton, Ohio. I obviously loved Aquanet. This is when my hair was bigger than my butt.

Standing with Mom before the Miss Ohio Festival parade, during my second year competing for the Miss Ohio crown. She sewed the outfit I'm wearing. You have to giggle at the parade hat.

I interned at C-SPAN in Washington, DC. I thought I had gone big-time!

Someone snapped this picture at our wedding. Our wedding had ten groomsmen, ten brides- maids, three junior bridesmaids, a flower girl, a ring bearer, and a lot of guests! That man has put up with me a very long time.

Early in my broadcasting career, I would wear conservative suits that made me look twice my age, because that's what I thought a news anchor looked like. This is in Columbus, Ohio. I'm standing with coworker and anchor Cabot Rea.

You're looking at the face of anxiety. You can't tell it here, but this picture was taken at the height of my panic attack problems, during my work in Chicago.

photographs, pages i–vi, courtesy of Robin Meade

Working at HLN, I've met incredible people—like country star Kenny Chesney. After this interview was done, he pulled me onstage during the concert to sing with him in front of twenty thousand people.

In a wind tunnel with the army's Golden Knights parachute team. That's me in the air! Way up there! We salute the troops every day on our show— yet I never cease to be amazed at the people in our armed forces.

Interviewing President George HW Bush on live TV directly after we both went skydiving with the army's Golden Knights for his 85th birthday.

This photo was taken a few years after I arrived at HLN.

8

THE BITCH IS BACK!

Let's Go on a Bitch Recognition Campaign

"What would you call a woman who confronts people?" Dr. Case's handwriting stared back at me from the page of my homework assignment. "That woman might be a…Yes! Go on a bitch recognition campaign! Write down the names you call people in your head." Index finger to thumb, I rotated the pen around and around in my hand.

If you write this down, there's a chance someone will find it and think you're a complete looney tune, the self-conscious part of me said.

Ah, do it! Write it down! Declare it! That was the daring, unlikable part of me speaking.

Okay. So what would I call a woman who confronts people? And my pen started writing: bitch, psycho, bulldog. *That should be enough. Okay now, what would I call a man who confronts people?* Jerk, pinhead, bully.

The homework assignment continued with this question:

"Where aren't you likable?" What an interesting exercise! See, Dr. Case was trying to get me to see that *I am* all those things I wrote. She wanted me to recognize where I'm a bitch. Where I'm a jerk.

At that time, I was subconsciously cursing myself for a number of reasons. One, my career path wasn't going the way I had imagined it. So instead of saying, "I'm grateful for a really great-paying job in a really great market," I said, "I'm working on the weekends." And I didn't feel the love or togetherness that I thought I should at work. In fact, I felt very much alone. Still, somehow I couldn't bring all that to the surface to say it like that, so Dr. Case wrote an exercise. My assignment: "Write down anything that you like about yourself and then dislike. It should be even."

Again, after a lot of inventory-taking, I had to write how those things both served and did not serve me. I drew two columns in which to write information, because I was trying to get the sides of my brain to go back and forth and make a connecting pathway. That way I might be more balanced. Instead of thinking, *I am good* or *I am bad*, the objective is to be able to say, *I am all of those things at one time or another.*

This is trickier than it sounds, because the things that seem obvious sometimes aren't. And you may not appreciate a lot of things about yourself until you're forced to do this kind of navel-gazing! So, thinking I was a negotiator and made people happy, on one side I wrote,

I like that I'm the middle child. And then on the other side I wrote, *I dislike that I am wishy-washy about Tim and me having*

kids. I continued going back and forth filling out both columns for likes and dislikes.

I like the talent God gave me to sing.	I dislike my impatience for anything from food delivery to painting ceramics. (*I want immediate gratification!*)
I like my abilities to make other people feel comfortable.	I dislike my shorter, meatier legs.
I like my abilities to be a creative writer.	I dislike my tendency to curse in anger at home.
I like my strong nails and hair.	I dislike my gray hair.
I like that I can paint walls.	I dislike that I let work affect my mood.
I like that I can usually think my way out of problems.	I dislike my recent jealousy concerning Tim's time.

You can see I was bouncing back and forth to attain more middle ground and balance. The more I worked on this, the less negative I felt about myself. Yet I didn't feel overly righteous, either. Which is the whole point of exercises of balanced thinking.

I like that I have the intelligence to usually learn things easily.	I dislike that I pick up extreme habits like using so much Carmex or going overboard with exercise and eating habits—I have a harder time breaking them.

I like that if I put my mind to it I can lose weight and get in shape fast.

I dislike that I can gain weight just as fast.

I like that I can anchor breaking news.

I dislike that I am not good at our new computer system at work.

I like the sound of my voice.

I dislike my nose, especially when it gets wider when I smile.

I like that I can be objective about people and grant them the benefit of the doubt.

I dislike that I don't have a backbone to make my cat respect my instruction.

I like that I can readily ask God for guidance or offer thanks.

I dislike that I am not a more steadfast example of spirituality for Tim.

Mind you, this is all just from one sitting. Dr. Case would usually make me do two-hour blocks, just thinking, working, and writing these thoughts.

I like beating the competition in the workplace or performance place, since I'm a bit competitive.

I dislike that I place so much importance on other people's approval.

I like how my singing voice sounds when I don't get

I dislike that I have a very hard time sleeping, though.

much sleep, since it's about
two octaves lower.

I like that I can wake up fast
and get going.

I dislike that I get angry
and stressed and frustrated
the more I can't sleep.

I like that I have knowledge
of music and contemporary
music history.

I dislike that I run late
often or always.

I like that I am a showy person in things ranging from
clothes to house decor: I
enjoy expressing style.

I dislike that I don't stay
in the present as much as I
should.

I like that I can make people
laugh and feel at home in
our house, and that friends
usually think of it as the
gathering place.

I dislike that I get so
stressed out before guests
arrive, wanting things
in order to the point of
perfection.

It took a long time and a lot of deep thinking from the
seven areas of life (financial, physical, mental, spiritual,
vocational, social, and familial) to sort out how I really felt
about myself. And then sometimes what I wrote seemed
frivolous:

I like my handwriting when
I try.

I dislike that I haven't
learned to swim.

I like that I can cook a couple of good peanut butter desserts.	I dislike that I eat so much when I'm baking or cooking.
I like my awareness of style and taste in clothing.	I dislike my round butt that's big for my body type and height.
I like my curly hair.	I dislike my curly hair.

WE ARE REFLECTIVE OF EACH OTHER

Once I got the knack of the exercises, I started letting go of the restrictions I'd originally had. And then I was willing to get into the sport of searching my perceptions—finding out how I was all of the things I had listed. That led to a bigger point: Dr. Case helped me see that with that integration, when I delivered the news, I could be *reflective of YOU, my entire audience.* You would be able to relate to me as a complete and complex human being, and I could relate to you.

About a year into our work we were talking about that and about my desire to land a job at the national level. Dr. Case saw it coming sooner rather than later because, she said, through these exchanges I had reached a point in my studies where people around the globe would be able to appreciate me on the air.

Then she surprised me by saying, "You have to see how you're a dictator."

I laughed. "Are you saying I'm like Saddam Hussein? Geez, Dr. Case, let's not go too far here."

"Just tell me, how are you a dictator?"

I knew the drill. But still I said, "Well, I'm not. Not really, Dr. Case."

"That's false. In what form are you a dictator?"

I pondered it some more.

"If I ask Tim, is *he* going to tell me you're never a dictator?"

I cracked up. "Well, yeah, with Tim!" I thought about the ways I refused to do our bills and insisted he gas up our cars and change the kitty litter.

Granted, this is not the same as being someone who suppresses an entire nation or rules by killing his own people. That's not what she was saying. Still, in some respects, we're all dictators of some kind.

THE PARTY DICTATOR

How much of a stickler are you for details when you're planning a party? I am the *numero uno* dictator when it comes to throwing a shindig at our house.

Our last big blowout was a WIG PARTY. I dictated that NO ONE was allowed entry without a wig. That meant women AND men had to come in headdress. I ordered twenty extra costume wigs to have on hand in case people showed up claiming to have forgotten theirs, or if someone couldn't afford to purchase a wig.

When the invites went out, it was the fellas who did the biggest whining. "This is going to bomb," Tim said, "because guys don't want to do it." Dictator Robin said, "Too bad! They can't come without wearing one!" We made sure to have so much going on at the party people would want to attend whether they were comfy in a wig or not. At the sight of the wiggin'-

out crowd, complete with a purple Diana Ross 'do, a B-52s-style bouffant wig, and many Rastaman dreads among the wigged ones, Dictator Robin stood back and smiled. Yepper, we're all dictators of some kind.

REFLECTIVE CONSCIOUSNESS

Dr. Case pushed me to see: "You're a dictator especially when you're reporting the news. You have to look the audience in the face. If you're just two-dimensional, there's no substance to you. Why do you think people come and go as anchormen and -women? When someone learns to be reflective and asks, *How do I see that other person in me, and how do I see me in that person?* they've found reflective consciousness."

I got it then. *Reflective consciousness* is a lot like empathy. It's about *not* being judgmental.

Dr. Case told me, "You need to see yourself in all the people you talk about—a dictator, a homeless person, a single mom, a president, an embezzler, a mortgage defaulter, et cetera. And conversely, you need to see all those people in you. If you can do that, then you can speak to a national and a world audience, because you'll own bits and pieces of all these traits."

Of course she was right. And when I could really think, *What's a dictator, and how am I a dictator?* in front of the camera, I would no longer think two-dimensionally.

"There's something about you that whirls, and whizzes, and buzzes, and vibrates," she said, "and people will want to look at you. They'll feel something, because there's something pure and divine inside of all of us that looks for a reflection of ourselves—someone who has already learned, and who can teach us how to love ourselves. Those are the great leaders of the human spirit over so many millennia.

"Now," she went on, "on the other hand, if you stand there in front of the camera and you're judgmental, you can't glow. And what people are looking for is somebody who glows—somebody who's magnetic. And you *can* glow if you can see life in all these different forms in *you*, because your sphere of influence becomes the whole earth. People will want to tune in to you all over world."

WHAT I'VE LEARNED: None of us wants to wake up in the morning and say "Well, I've influenced no one, I've affected nothing, I've contributed nowhere," says Dr. Case. At some level all of us hope to have an effect, and make a contribution to the world in which we live.

CONFIDENCE BOOSTER: You will have a greater effect and make a more effective contribution if you can see yourself in everyone around you. Tomorrow morning when you wake up, think about the ways you affected other people the day before, and how you want to affect, influence, and expand today. That's your ever-expanding sphere of influence. When you're done answering that question, you've bumped up your self-esteem because you're recognizing parts of you you've probably not recognized before now.

THEN IT HAPPENED: THE BREAKTHROUGH!

When she said those words, all of a sudden everything popped: *Zzzzit!* And I realized everything was in order. I was instantly quiet and humbled and my eyes filled with tears. I felt a warmth spread all over me, and I knew I'd had a true breakthrough moment. Dr. Case got tears in her eyes, too, and there we were, crying and laughing and feeling that good vibration!

Would you call that a miracle? I don't know. But in a way it was like Moses parting the Red Sea, because in a blink of an eye, my dream was right there.

Dr. Case helped me see that as soon as I acknowledged the intention to broaden my perspective with *humility*, I gained the power to realize that dream.

This dream was very much on my mind at the time because my contract in Chicago was coming to an end, and I didn't want to have to take just whatever was thrown at me. I wanted to be able to say "No" or "I'm going to look over here first."

HELLO, THIS IS CNN HEADLINE NEWS CALLING

And that's exactly what happened! CNN Headline News came a-calling, through a referral from a former coworker of mine from Miami. One day in 2001 I could hardly wait for Dr. Case to arrive for our session. I was all excited and I said, "Dr. Case, you're not going to believe this! I got an offer from CNN Headline News!"

Dr. Case seemed pleased, but not surprised. "Robin," she said, "it's prophetic."

But then the Chicago station where I was working offered me more money than I was already making, if I agreed to stay. *What to do, what to do—go for the national audience (or, as Dr. Case described it, "a bigger sphere of influence") or go for the higher pay?*

WHAT I'VE LEARNED: When negotiating, you can't get the best offer when you're infatuated, because if you're infatuated with something you're afraid to lose it. You're giving that offer all of your confidence instead of keeping it yourself.

CONFIDENCE BOOSTER: Get to a point where you are not giving away your power by being infatuated with the very thing for which you're negotiating.

"What are the benefits of losing both these offers?" Dr. Case asked.

Ooh, this was a tough one! But both Tim and Dr. Case helped me see what to do. Tim eventually said, "CNN Headline News is a great opportunity! It's national. It's cable. It's a fresh start. And I don't think your Chicago job is healthy for you right now."

And Dr. Case took me back to the concept of worthiness and loving myself. I started thinking, *You know what? That's not my last offer, and it isn't my first. I know what's best for me.* And once I realized that, I could go into the negotiation with a competitive spirit.

I could also speak truly from my heart about what was important in my life—freedom to be myself. And I could understand the limits of my tolerance with regard to everything from money, to travel, to moving. I was in a position of power then!

Dr. Case had been right all along. I went not just to a national network, but to a CNN network. You can see CNN Headline News (HLN now) all around the nation and in many other countries as well.

MY FIRST DAY AT HEADLINE NEWS: 9/11

Can you believe my first day on the air at CNN Headline News was September 11, 2001?

I was busy taping a show while another show was being anchored on the air live. When I saw the pictures being fed in live on our monitors, I didn't know what to think. *Is this a problem with the flight controller equipment—is that why two planes just flew into two high-rises? Why is this happening? Is this a terrorist attack?*

I felt my heart race. Like most everyone else, I wanted to believe this was some horrible accident, or just a nightmare I could somehow wake up from. The fact that I had to switch to newswoman mode helped me stay focused on the job at hand: to gather as much info as I could based on what was coming into the newsroom during those initial moments and the terrifying days afterward.

While the catastrophic events of that awful day threw the globe into panic, the anxiety that had plagued my own personal life for so long was subsiding. I was in a new workplace, and I had to focus on the news and what was happening to our nation, so I was busy staying in the present, thinking about other people and their lives, and not focusing on myself.

GRADUATION

A few months after I arrived at Headline News, I landed in my current role on the morning show. And it was in that role, I was relieved to discover, that my bosses were going to let me be comfortable in my own skin. They've been consistent and patient enough to let me find my way, reporting the news while also keeping my personality. When I felt certain my bosses would let me do that—and when I also loved *myself* for all that I am—the panic largely disappeared. Just as Dr. Case had said it would. *Poof!*

I continued to work with Dr. Case over the phone when I first went to Atlanta. But after a year and a half, when we saw I was able to think my way out of familiar traps, we decided I had graduated. And since I now have such a completely different experience in the newsroom than I had in Chicago, I have a much better mind-set.

In fact, many things are better. Tim moved his company to Atlanta and decided to lease space in an office building instead of working out of our house. And you know what? Our marriage got better, too.

Of course, I still have a few *quirks*, but they don't seem to drive Tim berserk anymore. And I have definitely learned to embrace my inner bitch! Tim calls the last day of the workweek "Meany-Meade Friday," because I'm a crab after working all week. But I can laugh about that and not say any one side of me is good or any one side of me is bad. There's a balance to everything.

Other than being tired on Fridays—and who isn't, in any kind of job—I've been extremely happy at work. What I do now, hosting *Morning Express with Robin Meade*, is very much on my life's purpose. I'm comfortable, and I hope the audience is comfortable with me. I get to bring the news to start people's day, develop what the audience sees in that four-hour block, and allow the real me to connect with the viewers, whether I'm doing a serious news story about New Orleans during Hurricane Katrina or cutting up with meteorologist Bob Van Dillen and sportscaster Rafer Weigel.

Our format allows me to be honest and real. I can laugh if I want. I can say to Jennifer Westhoven, our money expert, "What a bunch of malarkey," at the latest outrageous CEO pay. I think that translates to the audience as both confidence and authenticity.

Each morning I think, *This is who I am, and I hope you like me! But if you don't, that's okay, too.* And that's a big turnaround for someone who's been seeking acceptance and adoration all her life.

But let's talk more about YOU and YOUR CONFIDENCE.

The Takeaway

To get over a lack of self-confidence, you've really got to do an honest appraisal of yourself. If you go back through this chapter you can see where I had to do a frank self-appraisal because I had lost touch with the real me. Doing a self-assessment will help remind your brain of your potential and your talents.

Because the fear of not being liked was so crippling for me, I did a personal inventory of what's likable and not likable about myself. Maybe you've been in this position: if someone tells you you're not a likable person, it may be a stab in the heart. But when the pain subsides, think about that statement. Swing that pendulum back and forth so that you come out with a balanced way of thinking. And take personal inventory and decide how you really might *not* be a likable person and how that serves you.

How is it good for you that you're not a likable person? Well, here's one plus: if it's true, somebody running a racket on the street won't approach you, because you won't have SUCKER written all over your forehead. That "don't mess with me" vibe will serve you well all right! And then what the person said that hurt you won't seem so wounding after all.

Robin's Ramblings

Every good party needs a spectacle.

9

BE YOURSELF

Who Else Ya Gonna Be?

When you're all by yourself, and you aren't being something for someone else's benefit, what are you like? What are you like without the veneer of other people's expectations?

I'm not asking what the physical you is really like when no one is around. We have all sat around pre-shower on a weekend morning, marinating in our own juices. What I mean is that there is a constant of *you* that exists whether you're sick or healthy, abundantly rich or painfully poor. Those outside factors will come and go. Your health will ebb and flow. Your address may change, and so might the people around you. But what remains when you take all those things away—when you remove the physical and all those states of material affirmation—is the real *you*.

So why do we let all these outside things influence our confidence…if the very thing we are remains constant? Good question.

You are a constant, the same *you* from the time you were

born leading up to this moment as you are reading this book, and then past it until you reach the grave.

Think about it. Are you truly the job you do? No, of course not. You are certainly more substantial and important than the way you earn a living.

Can you be found in the things you own? Don't be silly.

Are you your spleen or your gallbladder? No, you can take those away and yet what is really *you* remains.

A GIANT INSPIRATION

At this moment I'm reminded of a remarkable man who lost his legs while serving in Iraq, but who went on to be an inspiration to others, including the New York Giants! Scratch that. He was an inspiration to the Super Bowl champion Giants! He helped them find their true selves as a team when no one thought they were the stuff of champions, not even themselves.

I interviewed Lieutenant Colonel Greg Gadson for a story as part of our morning show's ongoing "Salute to Troops" segment. The twenty-year army veteran described how he won the hearts of the Giants with a pep talk.

"I got my legs blown off. So when I come into a room, it gets people's attention."

Here's how the team came to meet Gadson: he had played football in the eighties at West Point with Mike Sullivan, who then became an assistant coach for New York. When Gadson was healing at the Walter Reed Army Medical Center, Sullivan dropped by to visit his old teammate. He was moved by the man he saw there.

"I went there to try to lift his spirits," Sullivan said. "And yet I was inspired. I just kept going back to how impressed I was with him, and how his story and what he stands for might benefit our players."

So Sullivan invited Gadson to visit with the team the night before they played the Redskins in Washington. Gadson says he was very much afraid of laying an egg in what was supposed to be his big talk to the team, which had been down that season. "I remember when my wife was driving me up to the hotel to link up with the Giants. I'm thinking, *Man, what am I going to say?* I had this dread of letting Mike down."

But Gadson's pep talk to the team was also a pep talk to himself: "I was saying I had to ante up and get my life back together." Here's how the head coach, Tom Coughlin, remembers Gadson's message: "One of the things he talked about was what it means to be a teammate. In combat, the soldier on your right and the soldier on your left hold your life in their hands. And you hold their lives in your hands. What he was saying was that when he was wounded, he knew his fellow soldiers would come to his aid."

And how did that translate for the football team? Gadson told them what they were trying to accomplish, nobody outside that room could affect. "If you can focus on that and on each other," he said, "then you can truly achieve something that is special."

It was as if his talk brought the Giants to life! The team responded by winning ten straight road games. By the end of that season they found themselves in the Super Bowl against three-time champs the New England Patriots.

It was time for Gadson to give another rousing message. "Tonight I speak to you as one of your teammates," he said in a straightforward but emotional speech. "And because you guys have embraced me as a teammate, I embrace you as men I would take anywhere."

If you know football, you know the Giants won that Super Bowl. And they felt so strongly that the amputee soldier was an actual teammate that he went to the White House with them and even got a Super Bowl champion ring.

Recognizing Gadson from the podium that day, President George W. Bush said, "He's got the Purple Heart, three Bronze Stars, and now he's got a Super Bowl ring minted for a true giant."

What a great story! What an inspiration!

But even after all those great messages of hope, one statement this double amputee shared stands out above all else: "I am not my legs, and my legs are not me."

Let that soak in. Here's a man saying, "My legs are not the *real* me. I am not just a person whose limbs are missing." Can you apply the same strong thought to yourself?

- I am not my income (or lack of it), and my income is not me.
- I am not my clothes, and my clothes are not me.
- I am not my losses, and my losses are not me.

In other words, these things and situations do not have to define you! You are so much more! When those things are gone, the real *you* lives on as a constant.

Thank you, Lieutenant Colonel Gadson, for brilliantly showing us what is so obvious yet so powerful.

WHAT I'VE LEARNED: Now more than ever it's important to recognize ourselves for what we are, not for what we do or have. Think about it: what's one of the first things people ask you when you first meet? It's "And what do you do?" It's usually an easy way to start a conversation or find out what you have in common with the questioner. Problem is, the current job climate has put more of us in the unemployment line than would have ever expected to be there. Many of us can no longer be defined mostly by what we do.

CONFIDENCE BOOSTER: Look deeper than what you do for a living to define yourself. I regularly tell people who seem starstruck at my job, "It's what I do, it's not who I *am*." What I mean by that is . . . we are no different from each other whether we have a highly visible job, an assembly line job, or, now, no job at all. Those things are external. They're not what's internal.

The Takeaway

You are more than just the sum of your experiences or the accomplishments you write out on a résumé. Your experiences shape you, but where you go from here is up to you. Your future is not dictated by your past. Be yourself. And live in the present.

Robin's Ramblings

People who are overly concerned about being perceived as the most intelligent are usually the ones who are not.

10

FRENEMIES

Feeling Confident While Fielding Criticism

"What routine are we doing?" I ask the head majorette.

The Friday night lights in the football stadium beam down, illuminating the contrast between the green grass and the white hash marks across the gridiron. It's halftime, and the other twirlers and I are in place, shod in short white marching boots, ready to lead the band across a chilly field.

She doesn't answer.

"Hey, which song are we doing? How does this go?"

She never even looks at me as she brings the whistle to her mouth. With a quick *tweet, tweet, tweet, tweet,* we're off, strutting toward the huge crowd on the stadium bleachers.

The camera bulbs flash. The spectators applaud and groove to the drumbeat. I can feel the large tassels on my boots swishing against my legs with every marching step I take.

We come to a halt. I still don't know which routine we're doing. And no one is sharing the info with me.

With the click of a drumstick on a snare rim, the instruments snap in unison for the mustering of the first notes of song. The music begins.

The other majorettes start twirling. I look around and realize the routine is as foreign to me as swimming without a floatie: I've never done it before.

Suddenly the faces of the majorettes morph into the faces of my frenemies, the high school girls who were supposedly my friends, but who I thought would rather see me choke on a chicken bone than succeed.

It figures!

I understand now: my frenemies dared to make up a new routine and not share it with me, hoping to embarrass me, leave me out, and make me thrash around out of sync.

Potty-mouthed proclamations start pouring out of my mouth. I can't help it. This royally ticks me off! In front of God and everyone in the stadium, I use the F-word. Two or three times. As a noun, a verb, an adverb. I call these charlatans bee-yatches. I make up a few dirty combos at which the crowd gasps, and hands cover mouths in shock. Then I really stick it to 'em: "If you won't teach me the routine, I'll make up my own! Screw you!"

With my head full of steam, I stake my own turf on the field and twirl into a torrent of tricks and kicks, designating myself the feature twirler. Honey, I am flitting about so fast, flicking that baton so high, and turning so many times before catching it in my hands, it looks as if the Tasmanian Devil got a hold of it.

The crowd loves it! They cheer for more! *Victory is mine! Applause! Success!*

This is how a recurring dream of my early adult years ended every time. And my interpretation of it is this: it is in the sleep-time movie of my subconscious that I do everything my girl-hood incarnation could not do—stand up for myself and dare to confront those I allowed to manipulate my feelings about myself.

WHAT IS A FRENEMY?

Do you have people around you who everyone thinks are your friends, but who secretly sabotage you? You know the type. They say catty and misleading things about you, like, "Doesn't she look great! Bless her heart!" (A beat.) "I don't believe a word they say about her having lipo!"

Or these so-called friends might be covert in their disdain for you, never offering an encouraging word or heartfelt congratulations, though you've shared the sentiment with them during their victories.

Let me take you back a few years. In telling you this, I don't want you to think I'm fixated on high school. I'm delving so far into my past because my lesson from the frenemies may be a lesson for you about your own confidence.

Let's jump in the time machine, replete with DeLorean gull-wing doors.

Back in school, there was a group of seven well-liked girls, and I was one of them. We were in similar activities, such as student government, National Honor Society, and band. So it probably appeared that we were a tight group who ran around together. The mother of one of the girls called us the Silly Seven.

Yet when I started to exert some independence with my choice of school and after-hours activities, it didn't sit well with some of my BFFs. Where most of them went out for some kind of sport, I veered toward the stage with drama club and show choir. (Thank goodness for mothers who encourage your independence! Mine said, "Go ahead. Do it! You don't need anybody to hold your hand!")

Most of the girls lived in town and could walk to each other's houses to spend the night. But I lived out of town and had a strict mother who let me accept only about a third of the slumber party invites I got, based on how permissive she knew the parents to be. (My parents allowed me to TP other people's houses, but that was about as wild as I usually was allowed to get.) Looking back, I think this might have been another thing that set me apart.

However, I soon got the hang of how to avoid the frenemies' judgment: if I didn't *tell them* about my outside endeavors ahead of time, I didn't have to be subject to their ridiculing of my goals. I got secretive as a defense.

CUE THE *MISSION: IMPOSSIBLE* THEME

Picture it: senior year, and it's the day before Huron County's Junior Miss pageant. I've been driving for weeks to Willard, Ohio, where the competition will be held, to take part in rehearsals. I've mentioned it to only a few close friends, and to the choir director who helps me prepare a song and piano accompaniment for the talent section.

I don't breathe a word to the frenemies. I don't let them know that I've been running to get in shape, or that I've had my neighbor sew a new citrus-colored gown for me. (Ooh, pretty!) In fact, I think I'm just about scot-free and able to compete without their jealous inquiry until...

THE PAPER COMES OUT the day before!

There, plastered across the entire middle section, are the contestants' pictures, along with a list of our credentials, our activities, and what we'll perform in the competition. Snap! Holy scalawag, Batman! Robin's been busted!

There was no way I could have beaten the frenemies on that one. My choices were to either tell them ahead of time and risk their snide remarks or say nothing and look schemingly secretive. What's a budding pageant gal to do?

My clandestine strategy did not go over well. One of my current friends jokes, "Robin, you have a strategy for everything!" And maybe my tendency to have a strategy also drove these young classmates crazy.

The newspaper article, while cause for interrogation from some of the Silly Seven, turned out to be a blessing. A number of other schoolmates showed up for the competition after they read about it. While small in number, they were loud in sound! I'll never forget the sound of my schoolmates whooping it up in the stands when my name was called as the winner.

Months later, though, when I traveled to Mount Vernon, Ohio, to compete for the statewide Junior Miss, I spotted one of the Silly Seven in the audience whom I hadn't expected to be there. I was so thrilled to have her there supporting me! What killed me about her was that she was a doll to me when the others weren't around. But when the rest of the group showed up, she seemed to have no allegiance at all.

We spent many hours together, and I truly enjoyed her when she wasn't going along with the others' mean-spiritedness. She had an easy laugh and a fun spirit. I can't tell you how many afternoons I stayed at her house in between class and practice or to get ready before games.

My adult brain knows now that she wasn't confident enough to stand in her own shoes. But my childlike brain just saw how she played both sides—confiding in me, trolling for information, then leaking it to the other side.

I wish I had seen that she didn't have the confidence to be herself. (I remember she couldn't accept a compliment well. If I said, "Your hair looks good!" her reply was always "You wish!") But when you're that age, all you see is, *She treats me differently when she's with other people.* Today it's hard for me to put her down, because I see I wasn't strong enough to even stand up for myself.

Have you ever seen the animated cartoon with the frog that dances up a storm and sings, "Hello, ma baby, hello, ma honey, hello, ma ragtime gal"? Of course, he only does it when just one poor hapless guy is around. When the guy tries to show off his amphibian friend to other people, the frog just sits there and says, "Ribbit." That's the way I felt the frenemies operated.

While the rest of the world was watching, they curtailed their conniving ways. Instead, they saved their jealous song and dance expressly for me. Super.

But there was one person who watched closely enough to catch the Mean Girls in action. She came to my rescue so often she should have worn a red cape.

I HOPE YOU HAVE A FRIEND LIKE JULIE

I was headlong into feeling excluded by the frenemies by the time I met Jules (my nickname for my great friend Julie) in high school. We got to know each other in typing class. Here's an image that time hasn't dulled in my mind: a girl with long curly blonde hair shows up to typing class. Her hair is still wet from the shower. She's tied it back with a piece of lace, Madonna-style. She's wearing a pleated skirt and wool sweater—very just-thrown-on looking.

It's Julie.

I was so impressed with what I perceived as her cool, I-don't-care-to-blow-dry-my-hair attitude. Nowadays she says her hair was wet because she hated to roll out of bed a second earlier than necessary. But to my eyes back then, she came across as half rebel, half artistic type, with her ballet lessons and plans to go to New York for fashion design.

Where I very much cared about other people's opinions of me, Julie, who was a year younger, seemed to have the air of throwing such concerns to the wind. Julie cringed when she heard the frenemies talk to me condescendingly. And she patiently stood on the sidelines until she couldn't stand it anymore. Finally, she pulled me aside and laid her thoughts on the line: "Robin, you don't have to hang around with these people! They don't even know there's a world out there! Get away from them!"

While I recognized their blatant cruelty, Julie pointed out how underhanded she thought they could be, belittling me with such nonchalance and subtle strokes of the knife that sometimes I wouldn't even realize I'd been fileted! Oh, that's gonna leave a mark.

Julie's words tore at me, because I knew she was right. But I was nearly paralyzed by turmoil. On the outside I was bubbly and upbeat. On the inside my gut ached.

As it turned out, one of Julie's classmates took care of it for me. Julie and I took anatomy with a girl named Stephanie. She didn't like the way the frenemies treated me any more than Julie did. One day the group really ganged up on me, and Stephanie surprised us all with her reaction. Suddenly she launched into an impassioned Julia Sugarbaker speech right out of *Designing Women*. She even stood to deliver it.

"You guys are just pitiful!" she barked in her most righteous, I'm-gonna-fix-your-wagon, Dixie Carter tone. "It's so obvious that you're jealous of her! Why don't you just leave her alone? You're pathetic!" It was her "and THAT was the night the lights went out in Geor-GIA" moment.

With that, she looked around the room, fixed everybody in the eyes for a theatrical finish, and then sat down.

Well, the room fell as silent as a tomb. You could hear only the clock ticking. Nobody dared breathe. Finally, the ringleader of the Mean Girls meekly said, "Shut up." That's all she could muster.

What a beautiful moment!

IF ONLY I HAD KNOWN ABOUT BALANCE THEN!

I need to point out that I was very unbalanced in my thinking about the frenemies. I saw them as antagonists who caused me pain. In my young mind, I saw myself as the victim.

If I were in that situation today, to become more balanced in my reaction to them, I would ask myself: *Where am I exactly like the frenemies? How am I the antagonist? Where do I cause pain?*

Interesting, isn't it? I've found that what I usually see as a fault in someone has to do with what I like and dislike about myself. Conversely, what I see as strength in others often mirrors what I think I see in myself, too.

WHAT I'VE LEARNED: Whatever you accuse another person of being, you are noticing that item about them because the same characteristic exists somewhere in your own being. Maybe not on the same level, maybe not in the same area of life. But the reason you notice it is that it exists in all of us.

CONFIDENCE BOOSTER: Next time you feel belittled by another person's criticism, recognize this: the same thing for which that person criticizes you actually exists in his or her own being, and is perceived as bad. You are that person's mirror for his or her own "disowned part"!

WHERE DID I RESEMBLE THE FRENEMIES AND CAUSE PAIN?

From the time machine again: as a third grader, I had a little cheerleading squad at recess. We'd line up in front of the high school windows because we knew the high schoolers could see us during their breaks. I was very serious about it and wanted only squad members with the best ability! I made all my little friends try out.

My friend Wendy wanted desperately to be on my pretend cheering squad. And what did I do? I told her she didn't jump high enough. Wow! Yes, we had been close friends since before kindergarten, yet there I was causing her pain. I know I hurt her feelings because she brought it up and laughed about it all the way through high school. The very fact she remembers it tells me that it affected her.

How am I like the frenemies now? I was blown away recently when a friend of mine told me she didn't feel support from me. She was under the impression I wouldn't be happy for her in her victories. (Isn't that just *exactly* how I felt about the frenemies as a teen? I was stunned!) She rattled off a list of what she viewed as transgressions from as far back as four and a half years ago! Quotes from me! Days that it happened! Circumstances and how they made her feel! She was truly hurt, and her hard feelings had become the eight-hundred-pound gorilla in the room.

I let her talk and talk. All I could say was, "I don't have any rebuttal, because I don't even remember these things that apparently are burned into your memory."

Isn't that just the case? Events that are so monumental to you and left you feeling so hurt and victimized may not even show up as a blip on someone else's radar!

And since my friend was taking a risk in getting things out in the open, I did the same. I admitted that some of the things she'd said or done had made me question her true intentions in our friendship, as well as her support of me. She, too, was blown away.

We both said we were sorry, even though we were never intentionally hurtful to each other. And we vowed to not let things build up for years before clearing the air. In doing so, we renewed our friendship with a clean slate.

Wow! If only I could have done that as a young adult!

WHERE ELSE DID I WITHHOLD AFFECTION LIKE THE FRENEMIES?

Truth be told, if I look closely, I can see where I even withheld affection from the frenemies. So what comes around goes around, right?

I got to be close friends with a gal who I'll call Aly here, who lived a few miles down the road from me. It was close enough that I could pedal my ten-speed to her house. I liked that house. It was big and had several additions put on through the years and held, among lots and lots of other cool things, the first CD player I ever saw. Ha!

Aly's family owned a successful meat business that eventually went national, with stores in every city. They were one of the few families regarded as wealthy in our town. I remember the first time I saw their two Jaguar automobiles in their barn. Affluence was so foreign to me that I had no idea what they were!

Anyway, I liked in Aly what I like in a lot of my friends—an independent spirit and a wry sense of humor. (I often say I'm attracted to people who can entertain me. Aly fit right in with that description.) We were so tight that for a while my Dale Carnegie thinking went right out the window.

In other words, I enjoyed our friendship so much that I

failed to bounce around to other groups and seek out other friends. And I left out the same girls who eventually became the frenemies.

My mother chastised me for it, saying, "You're ignoring all the other people at school. You act like you don't need them. But you need more than one friend."

Yet Aly felt like family. My cousin was married to her brother. Aly's family even took me on vacation one summer to the horse shows in Louisville where their sons were showing their horses. It was a brand-new world to me! And such fun! We ate out three times a day. We were allowed to stay in the hotel by ourselves. Aly was even allowed to go shopping with her dad's credit card! As Forrest Gump said, Aly and I went together "like peas and carrots."

But then Aly proclaimed she wanted to go to Harvard and needed a different education to prepare for that. So she moved away to an all-girls boarding school. My impression was the students there came from moneyed backgrounds and that there was lots of partying going on.

I stunk as a long distance friend and didn't write or phone much. But then again, neither did she.

When she came back to town to visit her parents, I couldn't wait to see her! But things had changed. I saw her at a basketball game and she looked so...different, so stylish, so high-class. I called her name, and when she turned my way, she did one of those look-you-up-and-down things. Was it my hair? Was it my cheering uniform? Worse, there was no hugging or "How are ya?"

Oh, well, maybe she's tired from traveling.

The next time she came home, she seemed so image-conscious. She never used to notice her parents' income. And things seemed tense between us.

One day the weather was warm, and Aly tooled around town in a convertible. A bunch of us girls piled in, and we drove over to another town to get some ice cream. And I noticed that whenever I said, "Ooh, I love this song on the radio!" Aly would abruptly change it. No biggie, right?

But to drive home whatever point she was trying to make, she really stepped it up: as we were leaving the ice cream joint, Aly pulled out and left me. Then she stopped the car a hundred feet away, as if to say, "I'm just kidding, Robin." But when I walked up to get in, she pulled away again. Of course, all the frenemies exploded in peals of laughter as Aly left me standing in front of the ice cream store.

It was deeply humiliating—so much that I would dream that I ran into Aly and said, "What's your deal? What is your problem?" That dream recurred for at least a decade. I couldn't quit wondering, *What did I do to her?*

THANKS FOR MAKING ME A FIGHTER

The pain of being left out and marginalized was excruciating for me at that young age. Yet sometimes when people are at cross-purposes, they still benefit one another. The anger and hurt that came out of those relationships were a profound driving force for my ambition in my teen years and in my twenties. Maybe they didn't *give* me my drive, but they certainly enhanced my need to do well and see what all I could be.

WHAT I'VE LEARNED: "I'll show you!" is a fabulous motivator in life. I've heard it said that many people who are in the public eye really have one person they are performing for in their mind, to say within themselves, "See, I made it. You were wrong." You know, the ol' "success is the sweetest revenge" line of thought.

CONFIDENCE BOOSTER: The next time someone expresses doubt in your abilities, silently say a prayer of thanks for him. He may be the motivation you need to get your butt in gear! You are only limited by someone else's views of you if you agree with those views. Agree not! Do not put artificial limitations on your potential.

Funny, in your head you think you're trying to prove yourself to someone else, but the reality is you're also trying to prove yourself *to* yourself. I just thank God that I eventually had the courage to be myself.

I can't say that the frenemies are still influential in my life today. But there's a good chance that when I went into my field of study—broadcasting—they thought, *She's crazy. She couldn't even get up and speak in front of class.* And the immature part of my younger self felt, *See, look what I did without you!*

It was difficult to see that silver lining at the time, because I was nice to a fault, and my way of dealing with difficult people was to try to kill them with kindness. I learned in church to turn the other cheek, and boy, I *really* turned it!

MOMMA SAYS

My mother, being in management, has always had little pearls of wisdom about situations like this. I came home from school one day and told her about a spat I'd had with one of my frenemies. I was licking my wounds, feeling really sorry for myself, and moaning, "I can't believe that girl would hurt my feelings like that!"

But instead of sympathizing with me and telling me things would get better, Mom gave me a fabulous piece of advice—one that has stood me in good stead all my life. She said, "Robin, you've got to learn to deal with assholes, because there's always going to be somebody who's a pain in your butt."

What a great thing to tell somebody in the formative years of life! She's right—there's always going to be someone who's the bane of your existence, and who seems to enjoy making your life difficult. Nowadays I can verbally stand up to people, and when I'd rather just wish someone away, I know it's better to deal with him or her. Otherwise that problem will just keep cropping up in another person as soon as my path veers from this one.

You know what's odd? As the years went by, I remember missing my high school classmates and wondering how they were. I didn't necessarily want to see a whole lot of them, but I remember saying a prayer for them often, just a simple "Dear Lord, if there's anything any of my high school classmates need, I hope I'm in a position someday to help them."

I went to my class reunion two summers ago, and only about three of the old group came. When I looked at them I was so relieved that I felt none of the same horrible feelings that had crippled me twenty years earlier. And one of the frenemies seemed to have no recollection of just how much time we'd spent together all those years ago. If she couldn't recall that, I'm sure she never realized the trauma I suffered from the way I felt the frenemies treated me.

DUST OFF THOSE GLASSES!

As for Aly, who drove away and left me on that strange street in a strange town, she started e-mailing me when I first started my job at CNN. I was really happy to hear from her. She's studying to be a teacher of special needs students. She still has her quick wit and I can see where she has the backbone to whip people into shape. She doesn't seem to put up with a whole lot.

After a little bit of e-mailing, I got up the courage to ask her about those old events that haunted my dreams for so long. I wrote, "You've got to tell me. Do you remember when you came back to town? You just felt completely different about me."

And you know what? She didn't remember a thing about that car incident, and she didn't recall being mad at me. In her e-mail she was like, "Gosh, I'm really sorry! I hope I didn't do anything that hurt you!" So what had been an atomic bomb in my life didn't even register on her radar.

WHAT I'VE LEARNED: That e-mail—and my class reunion— taught me an important life lesson. What we see as a boulder through our own goggles may not be even a speck in someone else's.

And the emotional weight that I carried? I should have let go of that a long time ago. Being balanced is such a wiser way of looking at the world. Besides, as Aly's e-mail demonstrates, whoever you feel hurt you may not have even known she was doing it at the time. Let it go!

CONFIDENCE BOOSTER: Try your best to let ill-intentioned comments roll off your back. Remember the line "It only sticks if it's true."

The Takeaway

Almost everybody is hypersensitive about criticism in some area of his life. But my mother really is right. You have to learn to deal with the jerks because you're always going to have somebody like that in either your work life or your personal life. For me, assertive diplomacy is the best way to handle it. Everybody has to find the method that suits him best. But I genuinely don't like to hurt other people's feelings. And I don't like for people to think poorly of themselves.

If we genuinely put ourselves in another person's shoes, we get a completely different viewpoint. And very often it's 180 degrees from what we imagined.

To get over criticism, try to look at yourself in terms of how it might be true, and then think about how it might *not* be true, so that you land in a balanced place. When I realized something that hurt me hadn't come from mean-spiritedness after all, it made me think about what I might have done to people without realizing it as well.

Robin's Ramblings

"No one can make you feel inferior without your consent."

—*Eleanor Roosevelt*

11

FRICK AND FRACK

Balancing Your Life

Let's face it. My mother, Sharon, is a character. She's recently started frequenting what are called "gaming rooms" in Ohio.

From what I can figure out, the slot machines are probably as plentiful as the arguments over whether it's legal to run or be in one of these places. She says, "They pay you in Wal-Mart cards or gas cards. It's not real money, so it can't be illegal!" Yeah, whatever you say, Ma.

But she's wise, as you've also seen. I still use the sayings she told me as I was growing up. They're just good, common-sense directives that almost never steer me wrong. For that matter, so are my father's.

OPPOSITES REALLY DO ATTRACT!

While both my parents come from Kentucky stock, in a lot of ways you couldn't find a husband and wife at more opposite ends of the pole. How extreme, you ask? Well, let's start with religion.

My father became a Christian at twenty-nine. He'd taken what the locals in eastern Kentucky call "the hillbilly highway" to Ohio to find work, and had subsequently met my mom. Her brother was married to Dad's sister (yes, brother and sister married a sister and brother!). Mom was eighteen and Dad was twenty-one when they said their vows. Three years after he became a Christian, he was preaching in the Church of Christ. He didn't accept pay from the church, even though he was in the pulpit Sunday morning, Sunday evening, and Wednesday night.

Of course, we kids were in the pews *every time* the church met. No excuses allowed. I can't tell you how many Wednesday nights I hauled my schoolbooks to the sanctuary to do double duty—listening to Bible study while I was scrambling to finish my homework.

Now you'd think my mother, being the preacher's wife, would be at the church door on Sunday morning, greeting all the parishioners, inquiring about their sick Aunt Gertrude, and begging to hold the babies. Truth be known, she doesn't even go to church with my dad. She's a very loving, ethical, thoughtful—and above all else—giving woman.

One time my father, exhausted with church work and disappointed in the fruits of his spiritual labor, quit church. Okay, it was only for about a day, but it was *she* who encouraged him to return, find another congregation, and continue with his calling. So I know she respects the man's steadfastness. And in my mind, she is a God-fearing woman.

Yet she will also call him a fanatic. I think deep down she

wouldn't mind being casually active in the church, but my father's all-or-nothing, black-and-white attitude would just be too much for her. Think about it. She thought she was marrying a race-car-driving, pipe-smoking, Southern-speaking hillbilly. She didn't count on being married to a minister. That came later, with the changes of life. And the duties of a minister took time away from the family. I think my mother probably wasn't happy. So she does not attend church with my father and never has. She's her own gal.

But you know what? As a unit, they balance each other out—even in their jobs, which was fascinating for me to see as a child. I had the union mind-set from my dad, and I got the management viewpoint from my mother. Tim says I'm definitely an amalgam of my parents, and I guess he's right. They both taught me the value of the workplace dollar, and how to keep my footing on the slippery slopes of negotiation. They also gave me no-nonsense advice on office politics—something that really helped me when I entered the workforce.

FUN DOESN'T PAY THE BILLS

For example, I remember negotiating one contract before I was married. I was working in a Cleveland newsroom, and I was rather disappointed at my salary. Then I got a much better offer from a Columbus, Ohio, newsroom. But I was torn. I kept saying to my parents, "Cleveland is a bigger market, so it's more prestigious. I don't know if I want to go down-market just to make more money."

There were other considerations, too. I worried how going to a smaller market would affect me later as I climbed the ladder. And I wanted to stay in Cleveland because it served the New London area where I grew up.

I walked into my parents' house with the renegotiated offer from my Cleveland station scrawled on a tattered scrap of paper. It was measly, in my opinion. On the flip side of the paper I had written down the salary the Columbus news director told me he would pay if I went there. It was *twice* what Cleveland was offering. *But what about loyalty?* I asked myself.

My parents and Tim (who was my fiancé at the time) all gathered in the living room. "I'm really having fun at my job in Cleveland," I told them.

"You have to go," Dad said. And then he gave me the most memorable piece of advice: "Fun doesn't pay the bills."

He was right. Most of the time, fun *doesn't* pay the bills. Now, I can argue that I've had a lot of fun and it *has* paid the bills, but for someone starting out, Dad's was good, practical, Midwestern, strong-shouldered advice. He was saying I should grow up and forget about choosing my work according to whether I could be on TV where my family and friends could watch. *But he was also telling me to recognize what I was worth.*

WHAT I'VE LEARNED: Every single one of us has an internal register of what her work is worth. If you allow yourself to verbally discount the products of your work, how can you expect someone else to value your labor and compensate you in a way that matches your internal worth register? Once during my cub reporter days I said in front of a producer, "I don't know what I'm doing!" It was an attempt at self-deprecating humor. But wouldn't you know she remembered my statement and brought it up to a mediator during a session in which the union and management were arguing about my title and pay?

CONFIDENCE BOOSTER: You don't have to be boastful, but notice the language you use when talking about your performance or projects at work. You may be joking or making a humorous attempt at modesty. But what you say, whether serious or not, could become how the other person classifies your work. Self-deprecation can be charming, but make jokes about yourself, NOT your productivity, at work. If you talk as if you're discounting your work, your work WILL be discounted by others. If you talk as if you value your work, others may be more inclined to value it—and you—as well.

Over and over, when my siblings and I were teens, my father would coach us that we needed to speak up about being compensated for what we deserved once we made it into the workforce. He said, "You have to go for it and sell yourself, and you have to have the confidence to make sure you get that across to your employers. Because they'll want to know what they're getting for their money."

And here's what tickled me about his advice: "If they say, 'What we really need here is a person who can do'—well, whatever," he said, "you just tell them, 'I'll do that.' You'll figure out how to do it once you get there."

THE BALANCE

I think my mother is a true conservative at heart, but she just loves to get a reaction out of my dad. That means she curses when she thinks it'll most bother him.

My mother loves to tell stories about their first grandchild, Heather. My brother, Kevin, and his wife were still teenagers when she was born, so my parents babysat Heather a lot, and you could tell Mom was a big influence on her.

How? Heather's first word wasn't "Mama" or "Dada," but "shit."

Once, in the discount store, my mother tried to buy her a pair of shoes and asked the tiny being which ones she liked. "How about this pair, Heather?" Grandma Sharon asked. "Do you like these?"

And loud enough for people a couple of aisles over to hear, our sweet Heather said, "Put that shit back!"

The lady at the end of the aisle bolted upright, then turned to my mother. "I don't think that baby likes those shoes."

Yes, the child had her own personality, right from the start, even if my mother *did* influence her.

When Heather was just a year and a half old, Mom had her at the house one day when I was visiting. And as toddlers do, Heather spread her toys all over the place. My father looked in from the kitchen and said, "She's made a mess and she's not even playing with those things. Let's clean this up!"

So Mom and I started picking up, and Mom said, "Heather, come help Grandma put your toys away."

But Heather just stood there, staring into the kitchen at my father. Then she looked him square in the eyes and screwed up her little face and called him the worst name she could muster: "Butthead!"

Well, Mom and I were just dying, you know, sputtering to try to keep from laughing. Dad stood in the door saying, "Don't laugh! Don't laugh! You'll just encourage her." I think it broke his heart that his sweet little granddaughter had just called him a butthead.

Looking back, I enjoyed a really balanced upbringing. I had Mom's wary, worldly sense and ornery temperament, and Dad's strict and straitlaced notion of how the other half thinks and behaves.

Who cares if it was a little schizophrenic?

The Takeaway

One of the senior producers of our show, Susan Jalali, instructs her producers to think of news programs in terms of a meal: "A little meat, a little potatoes, and a little dessert." Susan says the meat is the hard news of the day, and most of what you'll get, such as the stories out of Iraq and the national politics. The potatoes are the health stories or sports. And dessert? Those are the stories that leave you talking at the watercooler, like the one a few years back about the lady who said she found a finger in her fast-food chili.

I've found that human nature is the same—variety makes life vitamin-rich and makes us healthier by extension. That balance—in focus, in viewpoints, and in experience—is what makes up the kaleidoscope of life. If you can find it in yourself you'll be a more confident, more well-rounded person. But don't be afraid to challenge yourself to associate with people who are *not* much like you. Their diversity will likely teach you something and add to your own delicate balance.

Robin's Ramblings

Never trust a woman whose hair is bigger than her butt.
(I adopted this from a card I received years ago.)

12

BREAKING NEWS!

What Do You Want Your Life's Headline to Say?

Right now, in this second, think of your life as a headline, just like one you'd see splashed across the newspapers. What do you want your life's news story to be?

Asking yourself what you want to see as the headline of your *life* is a good way to take stock and set intermittent goals. You might surprise yourself with the answers.

Take Tim's business as an example. Tim is in the wireless wholesaling biz. We've watched his former competitors fall by the wayside or get eaten up by changes in the cell phone biz. They didn't diversify or make corrections to stay on the path they wanted to be on. Maybe they were too busy to see the evolution of the business coming. But Tim looked around and thought, *The field is changing so fast. I see my competitors going out of business. I've got to make subtle shifts so I can stay competitive.*

So he made some adjustments. He started two more companies within the same field, but with different approaches.

Now, instead of only selling cell phones, he's interested in how we recycle used ones to keep them out of the landfills.

In other words, he changed course slightly, so that if he wrote his company's headline right now, it would be ZIP WIRE-LESS STAYS AHEAD OF THE CURVE.

I looked around at one time in my life and realized if I were to write a headline about myself, it would be: ALL WORK AND NO PLAY MAKE ROBIN A WORKAHOLIC. My life was definitely a one-sided tale, particularly in Chicago when I would get up at 2 a.m., anchor the morning news, and then head out onto the street to report, sometimes staying out until four in the afternoon. I lived off adrenaline and the responsibility of providing a service to the community.

ROAD RAGER

My workaholic ways in Chicago nearly led me to a headline no one would want to see about herself: ROBIN MEADE THE ROAD RAGER. After a particularly long day I was fighting horrendous traffic on the way home. My pager went off. I assumed the producer had a question about the report I had left to be edited for the evening news. I phoned the number in the pager, but it didn't seem to be a number from the station. Still, I left a message: "Hi, this is Robin calling for producer Wendy. I'm a little anxious that I can't get a hold of you before this story hits air. Try me again. Bye."

Just then, I realized I was on the wrong street, driving into a dicey part of town without any knowledge of how to get out. Do you ever have one those freak-outs in your car when you're alone, knowing that nobody else can hear you? Between sleep deprivation, aggravation, and fear, I snapped! I cursed that car! I cursed that street! I cursed the city! In very colorful language! About that time I heard the cell phone: "If you'd like to replay this message, hit one." Oh, no! It had recorded me! I couldn't press the right number in time! Did the message get sent? Did it get deleted? I had this vision of the recipient sending the message to all the radio disk jockeys in town, and my freak-out being broadcast all over Chicago.

So I called that number again. "Umm, hello, this is the lady who may or may not have left you a message. Please excuse any curse words you may or may not have heard. And did I say I worked at Channel Five? No, no, it's Channel Two." (Only in those last two lines of this story am I being facetious!)

ROSE-COLORED GLASSES, OR GREEN SPECTACLES?

A beautiful thing about human nature is that even while you may take the responsibilities of your job seriously, at times you don't have to take *yourself* seriously. One truth I've learned through reading viewer e-mails is that everyone sees the world through his own glasses. In other words, you and I could watch the same news story and have completely different reactions, or even different interpretations of the facts.

Sometimes I can't believe the e-mails we get—especially when it comes to politics. We try very diligently to be fair, impartial, and equal in all our reporting. But a viewer may take one small detail and feel that it shows bias.

On our show, any notion of bias is banned, especially in political stories. We carefully consider the possibility of a viewer mistakenly thinking there is bias on our part, just because of a word choice, the use of a graphic, or even the fluctuation of my voice.

WHAT I'VE LEARNED: Now, think about my "glasses" analogy in terms of your own life and what you see as your own life's headline. When you become consumed with the opinions of others, remember, those reflect only the way *they* see it. Everyone stumbles around all day in his own little movie. Your experience may be completely different from someone else's, even if you were present at the same event. The same is true for other people's opinions of you.

CONFIDENCE BOOSTER: Why try so hard to please others when there is no strict barometer of what is good or bad? Let it go! You alone are the author of your life's "headline."

I've had to learn that point myself. Let me mention that we're fortunate that most of our audience feedback for *Morning Express with Robin Meade* is positive and edifying. We've built that kind of relationship by treating the show as a two-way street—we regularly ask for viewers' opinions on stories and their responses to questions about what they're seeing. We involve the viewer!

Negative e-mails don't bother me anymore, I guess because I don't let my self-confidence hinge on other people's opinions as I used to. Once, in Chicago, a voice mail from a Ms. Hadley left me in chin-quivering mode when she said she hated my pointy eyebrows and *Friends* looks. It makes me giggle now.

The fact that negative comments used to lay me so low is just a good example of how unbalanced I was about people's judgments of me, and how I had to accept myself before I could accept that not everyone is going to like me. It wasn't easy.

WALKING THE BALANCE BEAM

Any journalism student knows that the mark of good reporting is balance.

You might remember a story about a freakishly large wave crashing into a cruise ship. That sucker was seven stories high! It pushed passengers' belongings and furniture into the hallways. Some folks slept in their life jackets, and we had sound bites from anxious and angry cruisers. One woman claimed that while people were in the life jackets, the captain—trying to make up for everybody's inconvenience—announced the ship would be serving free drinks. The woman said, in effect, "If we're in enough danger to wear life jackets, do we really want people running around drunk?"

We could have stopped the story there, and it would have had a lot of impact. But to give it balance, we asked for a response from the cruise line. The company insisted the integrity of the ship's structure was never harmed. Even so, it hadn't stopped cruisers from getting off earlier than planned. That second interview, giving the cruise ship company's side of things, let the viewer make up his own mind about whether it was smart for the company to offer free drinks.

My point is that we need balance for the story to be right. And the same can be said of our lives' headlines: we need balance—between family and work, and work and play. If we have no balance, the headlines of our lives can get scary, skewed, and screwed up.

That's not to say there's anything wrong with hard work. Arthur Brisbane, a respected American newspaper editor from the early twentieth century, quipped, "The dictionary is the only place where success comes before work." But I can honestly say that even though my career has catapulted me from Mansfield, to Cleveland, to Columbus, to Miami, to Chicago, to HLN, I didn't feel true success until I found balance in my life.

IS SOMETHING MISSING IN YOUR HEADLINE?

You've probably heard someone say, "I have a great job and a wonderful family, but something doesn't seem right." In many cases we find the missing factor when we focus on other people's lives instead of our own. My old buddy Dale Carnegie said, "You can close more business in two months by becoming interested in other people, than you can in two years by trying to get people interested in you." It's true. When you give of yourself, you write your life's headline in a way that balances the equation of give and take.

Sometimes you may feel as if it's not appreciated, but you may be wrong. Let me tell you a little story.

When I was going through my anxiety attacks, I started learning different skills, such as how to decorate and paint walls. It was a way of both having a hobby and rediscovering parts of my personality that I had left behind. Well, a coworker of mine at CNN saw a redo project I did for another anchor, and said, "I'm next!" I asked, "Where do you live? Is it close to me?" And she said, "Oh, yes, really close." So I volunteered to do her interior decorating.

Well, she ended up living so far away that Cincinnati looked close! *And* she failed to tell me she had a wayward cat that preferred carpets to cat boxes. Smellavision! But I did it because I liked her. I had her walls painted, found her some off-price furniture, and sewed her drapes myself. Still, I thought, *Never again!*

More than a year after I finished, I had yet to receive a thank-you note. Then, one day, it came. And I know what you're thinking: *It's about time.* But inside the envelope was a funeral announcement for her beloved father. Her note went something like this: "My father came to live with me during his battle with cancer. He loved that couch you found for us, and loved what you did with the house. Because of your hard work, he was able to live his final days in comfortable surroundings. Thanks for making that possible."

That was so kind of her, and so humbling for me. You never know how your actions might affect the "headline" or monumental moments of someone else's life.

SAVING GRACE

Now, here's an aspect of balance we usually don't like to contemplate: losing. But let's face it—we can't always be the victor, try as we might. And to keep our balance when we do lose, we have to be humble. As my wise mother used to say, "You can't win the right way until you learn to lose the right way, and you must lose with grace."

During my days of competing for, and eventually winning,

the Miss Ohio title, rumor had it that another contestant was caught in the dressing room rehearsing. Not rehearsing her talent or her speech—she was rehearsing the *face* she would make when they called her name to win! You know the kind of look I mean—the feigned surprise—hands cupped to the mouth—followed by the smile and a tear.

The problem was, when she didn't win, she was accused of stomping off the stage in a pout. That's not exactly losing with grace.

I think my mother's larger point is this: there's something to learn from every situation, whether it's good or bad, pleasant or painful. That's a pretty good guide for keeping your balance when life tries to tip you over.

WHAT I'VE LEARNED: Devising a headline describing your own life is a great way to decide if you're on track now, or if your path needs some correction.

CONFIDENCE BOOSTER: If you're not on the track you want, hopefully you can handle it like an airline pilot. Did you know a pilot can make a huge correction when he veers off course with just a tiny adjustment to the rudders? By the math of angles, that small correction is multiplied many times over by the time the destination is reached. The same might be true of your life. Mouse-sized changes can have an elephant-sized impact on your self-confidence.

The Takeaway

You alone are the composer of your life's headlines. Stop thinking that things "happen" to you. Don't focus on what's beyond your control. Move in a direction of "making things happen." You'll feel so much more in control of your life, less like a victim—and you will be more able to compose the life's headline you sincerely want.

Robin's Ramblings

Don't take the credit if you're not willing to take the blame.

13

YOUR PASSION IS YOUR CONFIDENCE

(Your Compassion Is, Too!)

Think back to your earliest memories about doing something that brought you bliss. The world around you may have stood in amazement, too. Or people may not even have noticed. But inside you felt naturally drawn to this activity and were good at it.

Maybe it was the first time you used watercolors.

Maybe it was the first song you learned, and you can still remember it today.

Maybe it's the natural attraction you felt toward doing your doll's hair.

Maybe you realize now you had a talent for figuring people out.

Do you recognize what talents came easily for you, and in which activities you could totally lose track of time? For a lot of people, what they loved doing as children—what brought them feelings of confidence—ended up foreshadowing their life's passion.

As adults, we sometimes forget the importance of following

our bliss, because the tedious parts of our day take up *all* of our day. You know, the doctors and dentists, and the shuttling kids here and running to the grocery store there. But expressing your passion in some way will lead to all kinds of joy, accomplishments, and even new friends in your life—all of which will likely boost your self-confidence.

THE TAPE RECORDER, CIRCA 1979

When I was a snot-nosed tomboy I used to swipe my father's tape recorder. This wasn't a high-tech jobbie by today's standards at all. It was basic, handheld, with a built-in microphone and one tinny-sounding speaker. You'd jam your cassette tape in there and then flip it over when it got full, so you could tape on the B side. I think my father bought it to practice his sermons. When he wasn't using it, though, I came up with all kinds of novel uses for it.

For example, I set it outside on summer nights and taped the sounds of crickets and frogs in the wet grass. That way I could play those summer sounds back in the winter when we were all cooped up inside, and the long, dark months didn't seem so bleak.

I would also sing into the tape recorder and then listen, noting when I was sharp or flat. (I worked to improve, but still not everybody in the family appreciated my talent. When we would go on trips, the three of us kids would be in the backseat, and Kevin would call out, "Mom, make her quit singing!" Of course, talent will win out, and so will opportunity. So a little while down the road he'd yell, "Now she's humming! Make her stop it!")

Most of all, I used that little tape recorder to pretend I had my own talk radio show. How's that for foreshadowing?

While you might say I followed my passion and showed a propensity for my profession early on, precisely how I became a news broadcaster had a bit of serendipity to it.

WHAT DO YOU WANT TO DO WITH YOUR LIFE?

In my senior year of high school we had to take an aptitude test to tell us what we were good at. You know the test I mean. Essentially, it pinpoints what you already know—that you're either a science/math person, or an English/word person. Right? But it also helps point you in a direction for life.

Mine showed that I should have nothing to do with numbers, which didn't surprise me. I'm not exactly a science wonk, either. On the positive side, what this test did tell me was that I was good at creative writing, reading, and word comprehension. The instructions said: "Write down something in this field that you would like to do."

I scanned the page. There was no multiple choice. There was no list of great options in this field. Huh? It was just blank—and so was I. So I looked over at my little frenemy's paper and saw she had similar aptitude results. This wasn't a real test, so it wasn't as if I were cheating. I peeked again and saw she wrote, "I would like to be a broadcast news anchor."

Cue the hallelujah chorus!

I'm pretty sure the heavens opened up at that moment. *Aha! What a great idea!*

So I wrote down the same thing. And that's where my whole life came from. Can you believe it?

PERSONALITY PLUS

Okay, there was a little more to it. Growing up, I loved watching Cleveland news. As I mentioned earlier, during my high school and college years there was a news anchor there named Robin Swoboda, and she was the "it" girl. The bomb. Everybody either loved her or hated her, but they all talked about her.

She made an impression on me not only because everybody watched her, but because she wore high heels that shouted her support for the Cleveland Browns, whose color was orange. She'd spray-painted a pair of her pumps orange. I remember when she stood up at the weather wall so she could show the city her orange high heels in honor of the pro football team.

I also recall she'd often break into a laugh during news stories. It might not have been very professional, but hey, she was being herself. Maybe that's where I got the notion of personality on the news, too.

MAKING PROGRESS

So as I grew older this whole broadcast thing really started to percolate. When I filled out my form to try out for Huron County's Junior Miss, it asked, "What is your career objective?" I wrote, "My objective is to become a world-renowned broadcaster and follow in the footsteps of Diane Sawyer." My mom took a look at what I wrote and said, "Now honey, let's write something a little bit more realistic in there." She really hates that story, because she doesn't want anyone to say she didn't believe in her daughter!

That wasn't it, exactly. It's just that I wasn't what you'd call great at public speaking. So the idea that I could be comfortable voicing stories for other people was more than a bit of a stretch. And the sheer notion of a girl from the middle of a cornfield thinking she could make a living in broadcasting bordered on delirium. Even though Cleveland was just over an hour's drive, it was a very long way in the mind's eye from our small town.

But now that I've gotten over my reticence in front of groups, I see that my profession actually suits me. First of all, as you've seen, being the center of attention doesn't bother me. And when that television camera is on you and you're alone, baby, you'd better inform people and get their attention, or that camera won't be there long!

Therefore, I'm more daring when it comes to getting a story than I am about anything else in life. Following my bliss has created a perfect harmony between my work and my personality and natural bent.

PASSION IN ACTION

I have another story about following your bliss—which is actually another way of saying *following your passion*.

At Fort Bragg in North Carolina, we did a story that we called "Dream Jumpers," about two young amputees, both in the Eighty-second Airborne. Daniel Metzdorf lost one of his legs above the knee during an attack in Iraq. George Perez lost a leg below the knee after a bomb blast in Fallujah. They could have retired with full benefits and gone into some other line of work, because Lord knows it's been hard enough for them. But instead they followed their passion and reenlisted. They wanted to try out for the Golden Knights, the army's exhibition parachute team.

I went to Fort Bragg, where they train the Golden Knights, and I was impressed with these guys' attitudes. I asked them if they joke with one another. "Oh, yeah," Daniel said, motioning to Perez. "I look at him and go, 'You're not a real amputee. You're just missing a foot.'"

Could the rest of us be so resilient about a life-changing situation and retain that positive mind-set? You have to admire that they could share jokes like this with each other.

Our story followed the men through training, because we wouldn't find out if they actually made the team until months later. So there was that friction, that anxiety: would they make it or not?

As part of all this, I needed to show the audience what the "Dream Jumpers" experienced with a new center of gravity when they jumped out of planes. That meant I needed to get into a large wind tunnel with them, which simulates the rush of air you feel after free-falling. The goal is to learn to balance yourself in that amazingly forceful environment.

When you do this, you lie flat. Then the wind comes, and it's absolutely like a hurricane pushing you up. It was a great feeling, because suddenly I felt like a bird! In fact, the Golden Knights kept reaching up and pulling me back down, because I wanted to let go! But the higher I would have gone, the more out of control I would have been.

I can tell you it was difficult enough to keep my balance with four limbs and an even center of gravity. I thought, *How much harder must it be for them, missing a limb or a foot?* (At that point I was definitely following my passion to report good stories—I was really afraid of what a free fall would feel like!)

After watching the story of the two wounded warriors, our viewers felt incredibly connected to them. They regularly ask if they made the Golden Knights.

Here's the big update: on the second go-round, Daniel Metzdorf made the team! Isn't that exciting? He worked so hard to do so, when he could have just retired. Now *that's* finding and following your passion!

WHAT I'VE LEARNED: Without realizing it, you're probably attracted to people who are passionate about something. I don't mean the "I'm going to beat you over the head until you believe like I believe" type of passion you hear from protestors or extremists. What I mean is—we tend to be attracted to a person who shows us her bliss and invites the world to share. Think of an artist and her canvas. Think of the guy at the MP3 store who is totally stoked about his work! That kind of enthusiasm is downright contagious.

CONFIDENCE BOOSTER: There is something magnetic about a person who is doing what he loves. It's written all over his face, and it draws the rest of us in. Can you say you've found and are following your passion? It doesn't have to be in the realm of your job. It can be in another area of life. But being connected to your purpose is more illuminating than any makeup, plastic surgery, or special lighting could ever be, dolls!

EMOTIONAL CAFFEINE

I feel passionate about helping our audience start their days on a good note through our news show. Being a morning person is an outlook that lasts throughout your day, and I'm not talking just about energy levels. I feel like a guardian of your emotions when you join us for the news. In addition to getting the facts and stories right, I also feel responsible for what kind of mood you are in when you walk out the door. I see my job as that of informing you and getting you ready for the day, but also of helping give you the *confidence* to face the day.

Americans clearly have a lot on their minds that could drag them down, starting with the news itself. I think people tune in to us for information, but also for a little bit of an emotional caffeine jolt, and maybe even some virtual antacid to quell a queasy stomach. Our audience is attracted to stories that elicit real feeling, whether disgust, incredulity, or warmth. You're going to remember stories that make you feel emotion. That's what you're going to talk about at the water-cooler. It's another form of passion.

Because I know viewers come to us at a vulnerable time of the day (you're half awake, half dressed, and not sure if you should hit the snooze button), I don't want to inundate them with stomach-churning video. There are some stories that just don't pass our "cereal test." If you're sitting there watching TV, eating your cereal, and getting your kids ready for school, do you really want to hear horrible details of an awful tragedy? You might be ready for all that gore at noon, but your stomach can't handle the same types of things in the morning that it can later in the day. That doesn't mean we won't cover the news for you. We'll just be very selective about the kinds of details and video we put in for the morning show.

Now, what kinds of stories am I really passionate about? I'm attracted to health stories, because generally they affect a lot if not all of us. They're news that you can use. And I'm attracted to anything about the military—not necessarily to maneuvers or training, but to stories of the veterans, especially when they come home. Are they able to get jobs? What kind of medical care do they receive? Do we have adequate testing for post-traumatic stress disorder?

And apart from other types of news stories (like consumer stories, stories about people helping each other in the economy, and the stupid-criminal stories that make you go, "I AM normal, because the person in that story definitely is NOT normal"), I have to say I'm passionate about music.

AIN'T IT THE TRUTH?

A lot of people have been fascinated by neurologist Oliver Sacks's book *Musicophilia: Tales of Music and the Brain.* In it Sacks analyzes the astonishing effects of music on the mind, especially on the injured brain or the impaired brain of the Alzheimer's patient. We're learning so much about the pathways that music takes!

I often think about the programs that use music as rehabilitation or therapy. I can definitely see how that works, because I self-medicated with music when anxiety was a problem for me. Whenever I felt anxious in Chicago before the show started, I'd use music to distract myself out of thinking, *Oh my God! I hope I don't have more anxiety!*

My running joke with myself, even today, is that I'm afraid of my own thoughts. But I honestly used to be afraid of thinking myself back into another anxiety attack. So to stave it off I used positive songs as a mood changer. I'd hum them on the way up to the news desk, because music takes me away to another place. It was absolutely the soothing salve for my anxiety. (It's hard to be full of anxiety if you're singing "Walking on Sunshine.")

Music is an artificial mood enhancer. You turn it on and it takes you back to memories of where you first heard it. If I listen to "The Boys of Summer" by Don Henley, I'm right back in junior high school.

My uses for music on the news set today are different from what they were all those years ago. Now it's about keeping up our energy for four hours. When I first came to Headline News they didn't play music in the studio during the commercials. But we found an old CD player, and I was psyched. We had an anchor for high-tech stories about gadgets and gizmos at the time, and he would sit in the back for most of the show. I'd say, "Daniel, hit the U2, would you?" or "Press Coldplay, please."

Eventually our lighting director took over the job, and we got a bigger stereo. And now each lighting director who comes in knows not only how to light the set, but how to run the music machine, too. (Actually I think it's an MP3 player by now, and they just download stuff from the Web.)

All of us enjoy it, because when we're running commercials there's at least two minutes of silence in the studio. And on a four-hour show we have to keep our energy up, because there's a new audience tuning in every half hour. Many consider us one of the brightest and most energetic morning programs, and I think our use of music is one reason for it, since you can certainly find some depressing stories on any given news day.

WHAT I'VE LEARNED: Supporting a cause can magnify your confidence, because deep down you recognize you're contributing to the good in the world.

CONFIDENCE BOOSTER: By being involved in a cause or activity you're passionate about, you give yourself another way to answer the question "And what do you do?" You don't always have to answer in the form of your job. You *do* many things, and your causes and activities are included in that.

The Takeaway

As I write this, I recently sang a duet with Richard Marx in a concert to benefit cystic fibrosis research. (Remember his huge hits in the late eighties and nineties and his Grammy with Luther Vandross in 2004?) I felt honored that he would sing with me. But I also noticed how on fire he is for the cause of cystic fibrosis. CF is a disease of the upper respiratory system. And though it hasn't directly affected Richard or his family, he's been touched by the people who suffer from it (most of them children). What's got him on fire is that researchers tell him the cure is imminent, but that there's no government funding for their work. So private fund-raisers carry most of the cause. And that's where he feels he can help, so that's what he does.

What cause are you on fire about?

Over the years I've become involved with the World Children's Center. It's a planned community in Georgia for five hundred to eight hundred orphaned, neglected, and abused children. The man who founded the center, Don Whitney, saw an infomercial on television when he was only thirteen, about children around the world who were starving and hurting. It affected him so much, right at that moment he decided he'd dedicate his life to making a difference. That's led to the creation and the current construction of the World Children's Center.

Feeling passionate about a cause doesn't mean you have to hand over wads of cash. Your time and elbow grease may be worth more to many charities than your "green" ever will be. A better self-image awaits you when you give, in some way, to someone else, with no guaranteed gain of your own, other than a "thank you." (And sometimes you don't even get that.) Yes, my friend, compassion equals confidence.

Robin's Ramblings

"Without music, life would be a mistake."

—*Friedrich Nietzsche*

14

BE GRATEFUL FOR YOUR GIFTS!

Are You Taking Your Gifts for Granted?

If your self-confidence is down the toilet, you may not even *recognize* your gifts. Oh, I think I see you, sitting there with your arms crossed feeling indifferent right now, thinking, *I don't have any particular gifts or talents.*

Not true!

Aren't you really good at cooking? No? Me neither. Well, then, aren't you really good at eating? Ha!

No, seriously. In order to be grateful for your gifts, you do need to recognize them. And isn't that a good way to inflate your self-confidence?

Gifts don't have to be stage talents. They don't have to be athletic abilities. Your talents may be strengths that aren't showy at all—but that are still vitally important. For example, your given talent may be your ability to make people feel comfortable. It may be that you can repair machines or trouble-shoot computers like a pro. Or perhaps one of your talents is the way you demand your kids' respect just by saying their middle names and giving them "the eye."

MY TWO VOICES

I'm extremely thankful for the gift of my two voices. One of my two voices is my singing voice. It brings me joy when I use it. (Whether it brings anyone else joy I can't say for sure. Ha!) The other of my voices is my speaking voice. I'm grateful that I have something to say and the ability to say it. It's an essential part of my job as an anchor/reporter as I voice the news of your day and bring your attention to stories that might otherwise go unnoticed.

Of course, most of us appreciate something only after it's gone! And that was true with me. But just as in the big teases into the commercials we do on TV, let me say, "More on that story coming up."

BOOB TUBE ON THE BLINK

Okay, clear the stage for the "Boob Tube on the Blink" story, an example of how we are most grateful for something after we lose it.

In junior high I was indifferent about watching TV, especially our outdated furniture-style model that was the only working television in our seventies ranch-style home. It sat there on the floor and was so big the cabinet top served as a display case for framed pictures and tchotchkes. Yet it was still hard to see, thanks to a coffee table directly in the line of sight. Not to mention it only got three VHF stations and two UHF.

I was such a strong phenom of junior high flesh and blood that I told myself I didn't have to depend on juvenile distractions like *Punky Brewster*, *The Smurfs*, or *General Hospital*. (Why were the girls I ran with in eighth grade all atwitter about this Luke-and-Laura-wedding thing, anyway?) I didn't need television!

That is, until that television went on the blink.

Okay, I thought, *I can put up with a few family Scrabble tournaments with Mom and Dad refereeing the hair-pulling fests that erupt among us kids.* I also figured I could make it through a couple of days of Monopoly game marathons (even when my brother stole money from the bank and chucked it under the board!). *A couple of days of this crap, and the TV should be fixed.* Then we'd be back to watching fare like *The Great Space Coaster*.

My nonchalant attitude vanished after a few days. My parents were so impressed with the "togetherness" the family displayed without the TV (the Yahtzee at the table, the sing-alongs at the piano), they decided we would experiment long-term without the heap of twisted wires, the rabbit ears, and the remoteless control.

Well, I'll tell you what that was like. The cool kids at school (the kind who had *two* TV sets at home, and a VCR to boot!) would talk about *Moonlighting* or *The A-Team*, and all I could do was nod and go, "Oh, yeah!" because I had no idea what they were talking about.

How could I tell them my mom and dad had suddenly turned into the parental version of the "Kumbayah" leader at church camp? Togetherness? Reading more? Playing board games? What a bunch of hooey! Suddenly I very much appreciated our old clunker of a TV and was jonesing to get it back.

In my memory the agonizing "no TV" experiment went on for about half the school year. My parents argue it was only a couple of weeks. But it eventually backfired, because when they finally got the TV replaced we sat googly-eyed and gorged ourselves on *Gilligan's Island* reruns and *Alice* before falling into bed zombie-brained.

We sure appreciated the ol' set when we got it back!

Now, the irony, of course, is that I ended up making my living from television.

POOF! MY SPEAKING VOICE WAS GONE!

Our television was a *material* gift, a modern convenience and connection to the world. But do you have honest gratitude for your *innate* gifts and the opportunities life has afforded you? What are you taking for granted?

I became most grateful for my voice after I was in the position of losing it—once figuratively, and the other time literally. And though words are my stock-in-trade, I can't begin to express the gratitude I felt when I got my voice back on both occasions, because it was truly life-changing in terms of self-affirmation.

I lost my speaking voice when I was having so much anxiety. My voice box worked fine. It's just that I'd lost my ability to speak comfortably in public. And I wasn't sure I'd ever regain that ability after working so hard to develop it. Because of anxiety I couldn't speak for long periods on the air, so in that sense my voice was gone. And I didn't feel confident enough to tell anyone the hell I was experiencing. So in that respect I had lost my voice.

It was especially frustrating because I had worked so hard to gain the confidence to become a public speaker. It was easy for me to find my singing voice, even as a toddler. But it was pretty hard for me to develop the voice that allowed me to say something in front of people.

If I had to do so much as deliver a report in high school, as soon as I stood up my knees would shake and my face would turn red. And my voice sounded the way it would if I jumped into a vibrating massage chair. The frenemies giggled at my fear. I can remember getting up at an awards ceremony in school and having to introduce somebody. I froze.

The bottom line was, my inner voice that has something to say just hadn't yet developed and wasn't there for me to call on.

It bugged my father to no end, seeing this kid who could perform for people and be confident in that context, and yet wasn't able to speak comfortably in front of a group. He himself had overcome challenges to become a public speaker as a preacher. Being from eastern Kentucky, he noticed people in Ohio paid more attention to his Southern accent than to his message. And he felt belittled when Northerners would make fun of his drawl. So he got rid of it.

I'm serious! If you heard him speak today, you wouldn't notice one trace of a Southern accent. (Although whenever he gets anywhere south of Columbus, he turns it on like a light switch. Fascinating!) Personally I like hearing the rhythm of a genteel drawl. But he says he worked very hard to chuck the accent so that he'd sound like his congregation.

My father is pretty amazing. He had no formal training in writing sermons. But he just thought that preaching was his calling, as uncomfortable as it was for him. And eventually he *did* become comfortable.

So to me he would say, "Just be yourself, honey. Get up there and talk to your friends like you're on the phone with them. Just *talk*." Well, easier said than done, right?

It's odd, given this background, that I would choose to go into a field where I would speak in front of people. And why did I do that? I think it's because human nature dictates that whatever it is you don't have or you can't do, you want all the more. You might see it in a person who grows up without much, and then makes a big show of things later on—an impressive house, nice clothes, et cetera. You might recognize it in a person who grew up in an orphanage or who had a dysfunctional home life—his priority might be to have what he didn't have earlier: a happy family, complete with a successful marriage and children.

But this transition to finding my speaking voice was twice as hard as learning I could sing. In high school I was pitiful at both speaking and debating. And then I got to college, where I majored in broadcasting. That meant I had to not only speak but often ad-lib for an indefinite period.

I wasn't sure that I could do it. Yet there was something inside that told me I could survive in this profession if I could just overcome my fear of being judged. Yes, it was hard to see my talent at first. But I knew I had a natural tendency to ask questions like a journalist. And I had empathy for people and their stories.

Still, this career came as a great surprise to my parents.

"What? You're not going to do something with music—you're going into speaking and interviewing people and writing? Okay. All right." They were smart for not trying to talk me out of it. Another gift.

My first on-air tape in college is just dreadful. I'm scared to death, and my voice is really high like a Munchkin's. I sound like a robot. The show was live, going out to nine towns. I was reading the first piece of news I'd ever written, and I wasn't a good writer yet. There were no teleprompters, so I was looking down, and you basically see the part at the top of my head while I read my copy.

Ralph Waldo Emerson said, "All the great speakers were bad speakers at first," and, honey, I was *really* bad!

Today, when I do breaking news stories, I usually don't have the facts to call on, so I have to dance around the subject until all the bits and pieces come together to form a narrative. I remember my first breaking news story, in Miami. I just sucked. But those are the things that you get over and learn from because you gain experience, and you're not afraid of being judged anymore. And that's how it was for me to find my speaking voice. It was a real struggle, and I wanted it that much more.

When I regained my confidence after dealing with my anxiety, I vowed to be eternally grateful for that ability. I had nearly lost it forever, and now I say "thank you" to God constantly for my job and my voice.

MY VOCAL CORD IS *WHAT?*

Here's the story of how I lost my singing voice temporarily. In 1991 I was still in college, but I also had a job as a reporter at a local TV station. I'd attend class, then hop in the Bald Eagle—that's what everyone called my father's black Camaro, because the tires were so worn—and haul a video camera and tripod to fuddy-duddy assignments like the Shelby city council. I'd cover that for the local television station, haul butt back to my apartment, and get ready for class the next morning. On top of that I was competing for the title of Miss Ohio, so that involved a great deal of singing.

Well, sometime that winter I got a doozy of what must have been a viral infection. My voice was *this close* to sounding like Elmer Fudd's. Most of the time I sounded like the lady down the street with a three-pack-a-day habit and grandma ash on her cigarette. (You know what I'm talking about: she waited too long to flick her cigarette. So the ashes would be half as long as the cig itself.)

Anyway, it got worse and worse, but who has time to go to the doctor? I told myself that by the time I got an appointment, my sinus infection, flu, or whatever it was would be over. Besides, even with insurance I wasn't sure I could afford an office visit. I was too shy about asking for time off, too, because somehow I didn't feel entitled to time off. So I just kept working.

Meanwhile, the mother of all colds kept hanging on. I'd listen to my voice-overs on tape and giggle, thinking, *Ewwwww, my head hurts just hearing my stuffed-up honker!* Days passed, and I didn't get it treated. Weeks passed, and I didn't get it treated. Then months, yes, months passed. Ah, by now you know the routine. I just kept talking. And all that junk was sitting on my larynx, right?

Well, when I started to emerge from what I assumed was

my sinus-infection funk, I noticed my voice had lost its resonance. There was no depth to it like before. Think of it as the difference between listening to a song on AM radio and in full surround-sound stereo. All of its character, color, and tone was gone.

Worse than that…it HURT to sing.

I remember people looking at me funny when I'd rub my throat and say, "My voice hurts." They'd say, "Don't you mean your throat hurts?" And I'd answer, "No. My voice." I wondered if I was singing incorrectly, so my college voice teacher and I worked on it during our weekly lessons.

I also had an instructor in the radio/television department who gave me announcing lessons, to try to loosen up whatever had stymied my voice box. But I could tell something was wrong. And in my performance at my second Miss Ohio competition, I just couldn't nail my notes. My voice sounded "sick" and thin. I had no ability to "blow," as Randy, the judge from *American Idol*, puts it, dawg! No wonder I didn't win in my second try at Miss Ohio. It took a third try for me to win it.

After my second year competing for the Miss Ohio title, I was determined to find out if I'd ever get back my nice speaking and singing voice. So I went to the world-class Cleveland Clinic, where they stuck a tiny camera down my throat. The doctor and I both watched the screen to see the live video of my vocal cords. We watched the way they changed shape while I held out high notes, low notes, and anything in between. And what did we see? Two vocal cords, but only one that vibrated.

Hmmmm, is that normal?

"Were you sick recently?" the doctor asked.

I told him about what I thought was probably a sinus infection, and the mucus-run-amok sitting on my larynx.

Then he said, "That vocal cord is paralyzed." He explained that the other vocal cord was doing all the work because this one was frozen, basically. It was fascinating! Now I could understand why my voice was easily fatigued and why it *hurt* to sing.

BINGO! We have an answer! It was partial vocal paralysis.

But he couldn't tell me when the still cord might come back to life. There was no medicine for it at the time, although now there are more advanced treatments. He recommended I take a few weeks of voice rest and speak as little as possible. (You can guess how successful I was at that!)

IT'S ALIVE!

Flash forward about a year, to the day I was driving somewhere and noticed a tickle in my voice box. *Huh? What's that?*

It felt like energy starting to spark across a dead wire. Just a little at first. A tickle, and a twitch. It made me want to swallow hard and clear my throat. Then it would stop. It could come again in a few days or in a few hours.

And that's how my paralyzed vocal cord eventually came back.

Finally, I could sing my full range! My voice had its clarity back, and my announcing had feeling. Yippee!

I was so excited when my voice recovered. As a result of the months of pain, treatment, and worry, I do not take my voice for granted. I don't think I was ever properly grateful for it until I lost it. But you can believe I now thank God for it every day, especially when I think about what it was like to try to live without it!

Yes, I thank God for my two voices—my speaking voice and my singing voice, both of which I lost for a time, and never knew if I'd get back. Recognizing both of those gifts helps preserve my self-confidence.

Finding your own gifts and talents will empower your self-confidence, too.

WHAT I'VE LEARNED: *You need to recognize your talents.* If you do, you'll be thankful for your abilities and recognize them as blessings. This is a huge component to your confidence. It helps you recognize your individuality and develop your attitude of gratitude.

CONFIDENCE BOOSTER: Do an inventory right now of what you consider your gifts. Start with the obvious things that come to mind when you think of talents or abilities. Think about what others have told you you're good at. *Write them down!* This helps your brain recognize them in list form. Your mind's eye will remember that list when your confidence wanes.

The Takeaway

Taking stock of these things—little miracles, if you will—can help you celebrate your own happiness. And practicing gratitude for the things around you will help you enjoy a more loving disposition.

Robin's Ramblings

No divas or divos allowed.

15

YOUR VOID BECOMES
YOUR VALUE

When a Struggle Becomes a Strength

While you should be grateful for your gifts and talents, you also need to recognize where your void becomes your value.

What do I mean by that?

I mean that it's human nature to want something you don't have, to do something you're told you'll never be able to accomplish, and to try to achieve something that's a stretch for your natural abilities.

When I was working with Dr. Case I said, "Sometimes it doesn't make sense that I decided as a nervous teen to become a broadcast journalist. I could sing, but I couldn't speak in front of people."

She said, "It's a classic case of your void becoming your value."

Isn't that just the most wonderful phrase? Often we want something *so much* because we don't think we can ever feel it in our grasp. That's been etched in my brain ever since.

VALUE HAS A DOUBLE MEANING

If you really look at the word *value*, Dr. Case's statement takes on a double meaning:

First, your void becomes your value, with *value* meaning an emotional currency. You *value* whatever you can't do so much that you overcome your limitations to achieve it.

Second, your void becomes your value, with *value* meaning it becomes the way you make a living, the way you define yourself. Your *void* is the very thing that you overcome, to such a level that it becomes your strength, your *value*.

For example, James Earl Jones stuttered as a child. He pretended to be mute at school and insisted on communicating only in writing, according to the American Academy of Achievement's biography of him. Now he's this great actor, using his voice to help bring his characters to life. His deep voice is part of CNN forever. ("THIS...is CNN.")

I probably wanted to succeed so badly in television news because I wasn't sure I could master it. That was the void, so therefore I ascribed a lot of value to it. In the end my void also ended up being my value in the sense that it's how I make my living. It's what makes me stand out in a crowd, so to speak.

Why are we drawn to such challenges? Well, I'm not a psychologist, and it would probably take someone with that kind of training to answer that question fully. But when we achieve our goals, when the void-value equation gets righted, we naturally have increased confidence. We worked hard, beat out the competition, and saw all that we could be. We did it! Hurrah!

But to do so, first we have to identify what those voids and values are, and that often takes some soul-searching.

FORMER HOSTAGES IN COLUMBIA

I got to see the results of such soul-searching in some amazing men.

In 2003 the surveillance plane of three US military contractors crashed in the southern Columbian jungle. For five long years the Marxist rebel group FARC held these men hostage. After their capture, little was known about the contractors' whereabouts, or the barbaric conditions they lived under for so long.

When the hostages were freed in July 2008 in a bold and brazen commando rescue, every journalist wanted to be the one to tell their story.

About that time, I was clackety-clack-clacking through the hallways of CNN Center in my high heels after a particularly busy day. I had already anchored four hours on the air, then taped *Accent Health*, a show that runs in doctors' offices.

My BlackBerry was vibrating, indicating I had incoming e-mail. It was from my boss, asking me to go see him before I left the office that day.

Great. What did I do wrong? (And why is it that when we get called to the principal's office, we think the worst? Ha!)

When I breezed into his office, my boss looked up and said, "You, Anderson Cooper, and Larry King are up for this interview with the three Columbian hostages."

If I remember correctly, my reply was something cool: "Huh, no kidding." I was floored, because I hadn't made any calls to get the interview. But I didn't want to act as if I hadn't been to the big game before. I stammered, "I'm really glad I'm up for it."

It was a short time before I learned the hostages decided to grant their first exclusive interview to me.

Why did Tom Howes, Keith Stansell, and Marc Gonsalves choose me? I can't be sure. But I think a couple of things may have come into play.

For one, they were staying on a military base, and our "Salute to Troops" segment is obviously popular with the military. This is a shout-out we give to service members every day on our show, because it doesn't matter how you feel about any mission or any political party. These men and women are making a sacrifice. The least we can do is show gratitude for those serving our country.

Anyway, the hostages were being assimilated back into society through a program at Fort Sam Houston in San Antonio. I'd already been there, shooting other "Salute to Troops" segments, so many of the military personnel were already familiar with our show. It's possible one of them told the former hostages that I was a sensitive interviewer.

I'd heard that these men were very uncomfortable with the idea of doing the interview, and that if they didn't like the way it was going the interview could end on a dime. So there was a lot of pressure.

But also on my side was the worldwide reach of the CNN family of networks, of which HLN is a part. I think the men may have watched our show for a few days before the interview and felt I would treat them respectfully. Whatever the reason for the decision, I was deeply honored.

In preparing for the interview I decided to start with the dramatic and stunning story of their rescue, because that was the most recent event, and they would be able to remember it with great detail. But I also wanted to begin there because it was a happy time, and I could ease them into talking about the horrors of captivity. Can you imagine the emotional toll of being locked up at night, with chains around your neck while you sleep?

For men who had lived under a canopy of leaves for five years, who had been caged, had suffered malaria, and had been forced to march through the jungle for twenty-four days straight, weighted down with excruciating loads, they were astonishingly normal and well-adjusted.

I asked them how they had survived it all, especially the isolation, since they were ordered not to speak or communicate in any way for months at one point. In haunting detail, they launched into their story.

"I remember my darkest day was in the first months of our captivity," Marc told me. "We were, at that point, locked in boxes at night. And they would unlock the boxes to let us out. One night I dreamed about my daughter, my little girl. And this dream was so real. She was sitting on my lap, and she had little braids in her hair. And it was a wonderful dream with all of my family. But the problem was I woke up.

"And being freshly abducted, it hurt. It was very, very painful. I couldn't lift my chin. My head got so heavy. We weren't allowed to speak to each other at that time. But Keith saw from the other corner of the camp that I was in a very hard, difficult moment. And these two guys came over, and they put their arms around me. When they did that, I just started bawling. It was a hard, hard day. I cried a lot."

To keep their wits, they looked for any way to exercise their brains and mentally made up list upon list to keep their minds sharp. One of them planned how he would build an entire house. The others, feeling as if they'd dropped out of the Information Age, drooled over a computer ad they saw in a newspaper. ("We were trying to school ourselves, thinking, what is this?")

And Marc achieved the astonishing, spending three months carving an entire set of chess pieces—knights, queens, kings, you name it—with a broken piece of machete and whatever wood he could find. He'd sit there every day and work on it.

Technically he was not allowed to use his hands for anything. But some of the lower-ranking guards wanted to see if he could do it. He made the chessboard out of a piece of cardboard, drawing perfect squares. Then he sealed the entire board with clear tape, so nothing in the jungle—not the rain, the dampness, or the bugs—could penetrate it.

When he was finished, both the hostages and their captors played hundreds of hours on it. That thing survived years in the jungle and hours of play. I know, because they brought it to the interview, and they were so proud of what Marc had been able to do.

FROM HOSTAGES TO HEROES

The remarkable and heroic stories of Tom Howes, Keith Stansell, and Marc Gonsalves can be viewed as illustrating the void-value equation.

Their void was that they didn't have freedom to do what they wanted. They couldn't go home. They were physically hostage to rebels. Because of that void they achieved excellence at keeping their minds free. Though their bodies were in captivity, their minds became their place of action—more free than ever in their lives. Their ability to freely imagine allowed them to compile detailed lists in their lively brains. In the camps, staying mentally agile and sharp became their value. As Keith said about playing chess, "When you're doing that, you're free. Your mind is engaged. You are not a prisoner. And that's the game, that's the victory, and they don't even know it."

During those harsh, harrowing years, these men reevaluated their lives. A distinct void—their closeness and participation with their families—became one of the values they appreciated most. In our interview they said they realized that up until the time they were taken hostage, they had neglected one enormous piece of their lives—their families. And as they sat there thinking day in and day out in the jungle, that was the void that pained them the most.

Tom said, "Before, I was a typical American guy who was busy working [and] running through life full speed. I had a wife and a little boy that was five years old. Another one fifteen. We'd just got a house, and I had twelve nights in the house of my dreams.

"I've had a lot of time to reflect on my failures [and] my

successes, and beat up everything I have done. The three of us know better than any of you guys out there [that] the most important thing is the thinking about the kids, the wives, Mom and Dad. We forget that when we're going full speed…Now I've got lists of marriage hints."

His fellow American hostages gave him relationship tips during the years they were all forced to remain in the jungle. That way, once they returned to civilization Tom would know how to manage his family relationships better.

Marc had been "very motivated for the mission and my job" before the crash. "Because of that, I didn't spend as much time with my family as I would have liked. I was a normal American. I loved my country. But I took things for granted. Who I am now is even more of a family man who will spend as much time as I can with my children. And who loves my country more than ever."

Keith, who learned he has five-year-old twin boys, said his thoughts were parallel to Tom's. "I'm a person who has redefined my values system. We all now have an appreciation for the smallest thing. A cold glass of water. Just seeing your kid's photo. Or a phone call from your mom, in Marc's case. And hopefully, it never leaves me."

Each of the former FARC hostages now has a chance to live his life backward, in a sense, in that he saw what he wanted to do over and do better. I wish them every success!

Conducting that interview was the opportunity of a lifetime and a huge feather in my professional cap. But more than that, I don't know that I have ever covered a news story that affected me more. The resilience of Tom Howes, Keith Stansell, and Marc Gonsalves is nothing short of amazing, and I will never forget those brave men.

THE SELFLESS TROOPS AND THEIR
SELFLESS SPOUSES

Our "Salute to Troops" reports have brought me in contact with so many extraordinary men and women.

At Fort Bragg, for example, we did a story on a woman named Wesley, whose husband was serving as a major with the Eighty-second Airborne in Afghanistan. The major had told her about his patrols as part of Operation Enduring Freedom and mentioned to her that the children in Afghanistan were fascinated by the service members' pens. To help her husband on his daily missions, Wesley started the Pens for Progress program—a sort of pen and pencil drive—at the elementary school her daughters attended. That way the men could use pens, pencils, construction paper, and small toys to make friends with the Afghan children and give them hope where they had had none under Taliban rule.

Talk about a void becoming a value!

Well, the American kids brought in buckets and buckets of pencils, markers, gel pens, crayons—you name it. And when I went to this school to tape the story at Fort Bragg, they were so happy to show me what they had collected for the children of Afghanistan.

We took the tapes back to Atlanta to put the story together, and then we returned for Memorial Day to present these stories live for the show from Fort Bragg. But we learned that in the mere fourteen days that had passed between our taping of the story and the live show, Wesley's husband had been killed in action.

I kept thinking about Wesley and her two tiny girls, who sat in on the taping with the other children thinking that these pens would go to their daddy and his men.

We said to Wesley, "We don't have to run your story if this is too painful for you. We can pull it."

But she insisted we go ahead and air it with no changes. Her sentiment was, "We were doing this for my husband, and this is what he believed in." So in accordance with her wishes the story ran. But it was so sad when we added a tag to the story, telling the audience about her husband's passing.

Wesley's selflessness, even amid heartache, was terribly moving. I could only imagine her grief and confusion in dealing with issues like memorials, insurance, and wills. And yet she wanted to make sure her tragedy didn't overshadow the effort to help the kids in Afghanistan.

I'm regularly just as impressed by the families of troops as I am by the troops themselves. And when you think about it, the families don't get much attention or praise for their sacrifices. And they show so much support day in and day out. That story, like so many others, sticks with me.

NEVER, EVER COUNT ANYBODY OUT!

The saga of Kevin Everett, a tight end for the Buffalo Bills, is a different application of the void-value equation, but no less courageous. On September 9, 2007, in the first week of the 2007 NFL season, Everett attempted to tackle Denver Bronco Domenik Hixon and sustained a life-threatening cervical spine injury. He was carried off the field by an ambulance, underwent emergency surgery, and was put on a respirator to breathe. Doctors believed he had sustained permanent neurological impairment and would be paralyzed for life.

But if you're Kevin Everett and you're told you will never walk again, then by George, you're going to prove them wrong.

Do you see how his void became what he valued?

A mere two months after his injury, he walked in public for the first time in the Bills' home finale against the New York Giants. And on January 31, 2008, he appeared on *Oprah*, walking under his own power. He's never going to play football again—the Bills eventually cut him from the team so he could receive full lifetime disability—but he's quite the *Sports Illustrated* story. Again, Kevin's void became his value, because he wanted it more than anything.

THIS BIRD HAS FLOWN

I started taking pilot lessons last year. Why am I trying to fly? There are a couple of reasons. One, I believe you should do what scares you the most, because if you want to experience an authentic rush of adrenaline, that's the way to do it. Besides, then you will have conquered your fear. Chalk it up to another void becoming a value!

Keep in mind, though, you're talking about a white-knuckled traveler. I'd rather volunteer for an experimental proctologic exam, followed by cleaning the crud off a crusty commode, than fly cross-country crammed in coach. Especially after being felt up at security!

I've never been a fan of flying. And after 9/11 I was *really* not a fan of flying. When I told Dr. Case I was taking pilot lessons she said, "What a beautiful metaphor for you! You're seeing everything you've been through from above, and rising above it."

Hey, I guess that's true! I hope so, anyway. My thinking is this: learning to fly can be a real value to me. I can overcome the uneasiness I feel at every ding and squeak a plane makes during a commercial flight. You know that glance you give the person across the aisle, the "Did you hear that and does it frighten you" look, followed by the "Well if you don't look concerned then I'll just go back to these odd tasting peanuts" expression? By taking pilot lessons, I think I'll feel a lot more comfortable. I'll know what they're doing in the cockpit, and if the plane takes a little dip I'll know exactly what that is.

But the greatest value I see in all this is being able to use the information I'll learn on the air. If I have a pilot's license I can talk more knowledgeably about aerodynamics. As a news anchor you're unfortunately thrown into the position of anchoring a lot of no-landing-gear stories. Or even worse, stories about plane crashes with a number of fatalities. When I worked in Chicago I was nominated for a regional Emmy for my report on how to decrease the chances of injury in survivable plane crashes. So it's a subject that interests me both personally and professionally.

Remember when it seemed as if every other day we were watching planes coming in for emergency landings live on the air? I'll never forget the story of the JetBlue passengers who had the satellite TV on board, and watched the coverage of their own emergency landing live! Talk about gutsy, yikes!

Anyway, my feeling is that we have such huge numbers of

planes in the air every day, and such a huge national interest in aviation, that it can only be beneficial for me to understand the science of flight, the parts of a plane, and the ins and outs of being a pilot.

MY PROGRESS REPORT

At this writing I've had only a few lessons. I was exhausted after the first one because I had been so nervous. Of course, with flight lessons you're the pilot and you have control, but the copilot also has control. So if I were ever really in trouble, the flight instructor could correct it. He or she is not going to let you go so far that you crash a plane, right?

The first thing I learned was to taxi. (You do this with just your feet and legs.) It was exhilarating, but the instructor wanted me to look around. And man, my eyes were right there on the horizon! I was ramrod-straight, and I was going to keep that plane straight, too. But I was tickled because he said, "You show a talent for this." So I did a takeoff, and I think he was even going to let me land the plane, too. I said, "Ohhhh no! You're taking this plane and you're landing it! I'm beat."

With my second lesson I felt a little bit more secure. I'd done some book work and video work and gotten past some of the things that scared me most. I know now that planes come with built-in stability. They don't fall out of the sky because of turbulence, for example. Now I seem to be more worried about mechanical problems. That's a void, feeling uncomfortable on airliners. But as a budding pilot, I'm most afraid of getting into an accidental spin or stall.

One of the directors of our news show, Tom Gaut, and his

wife went out to the field with me for my first lesson, and they kept saying, "I can't believe Tim's not here!" I said, "Well, Tim's not here because he said he doesn't like the way I drive, so he sure as hell wasn't going to like the way I fly."

Tim feels about flying the same way I feel about his riding his motorcycle. You care for the safety of the person you love, that's all. But I want to keep doing things that add value to my life experience. You only go around once!

WHAT I'VE LEARNED: Your challenges today are very likely the struggles that help you develop strength and gain success tomorrow. In other words, we need to be grateful for things that suck now!

CONFIDENCE BOOSTER: Think of where your void has become your value. By recognizing this, you'll help your brain understand that even something painful can have its benefits. You're helping yourself realize you can overcome many challenges and build them into strengths. Use this to bolster your confidence when you feel as though you cannot overcome.

YOU MIGHT NEED SOME HELP

When home values started to increase in the late nineties, it was the in thing to start making improvements to your home to add value to it. Retile the floor! Add an artsy backsplash! Paint a faux finish!

DIY (do it yourself) decor was intriguing to me, especially the part where you didn't have to pay someone else to make your home look pretty. But I had no idea where to start! Talk about a void.

One Saturday night, when we lived in Chicago, I got a decorating itch that needed scratching. I'd spent the entire afternoon watching home-decorating shows while cleaning the house, getting ready for brunch guests who were arriving the next morning. The man was a big-timer at Motorola in Chicago, and his wife had done a great job decorating their home. So I was feeling some pressure.

Funny thing about those decorating TV shows—they make every home project look as if you go from start and finish in one half hour. The hosts pop open the paint can, roll on the new color (never dripping on the carpet), and zip-a-dee-doo-dah, they're done!

Suddenly that evening, I got the idea that *we must sponge-paint the powder room.* Tim said, "Oh, really? You've never done anything like that before, so how are you going to do that?"

"I don't know, but it can't be hard. I got paint, I got a sponge, let's do it!"

I remember *not* taping off the parts of the wall and wood trim I didn't want covered in paint (a doozy of a DIY no-no). I also remember not even fathoming my color choices. I just knew I had maroon paint in the basement, and I was going to use it.

Well, you can guess what a disaster this whole thing was, right? The sponge I was using was wet, so the paint mixed with the water of the sponge and began to run down the wall. What was supposed to look like little flecks of color started looking like streams of blood. When I stepped back to see my work, I could do nothing but stare in frustration. It looked like the scene of a mass murder with red splatters across the walls!

My hubby was right. I didn't know what I was doing.

"Tim, you've got to help me with this! You've got to paint white over it before they come tomorrow. Please!"

Poor Tim got up early on Sunday and did it, and we told our guests the whole story. By that time it was hysterical, and in the retelling it sounded like an episode of *I Love Lucy*.

After the guests had left and the dishes were washed, Tim cleared the air: "Never again! You're going to take a painting class and know what you're doing before you do this again! You're not going to practice on the walls of the house!"

Guess he was putting his foot down.

I didn't know how, but I knew I wanted to make our home a beautiful and comfortable place to be without hiring someone else to do it.

A few years later, when we moved to downtown Chicago, I got the decorating bug again. But this time I took a faux-finishing painting class. And I was the star of my class! My work was good! Then I used the same effects I'd learned in class on the walls of my home, and I earned rave reviews! The effects added visual appeal to our home and came into play when we sold it.

When we moved to Atlanta I graduated to another aspect of decor: window dressings. My mom came to visit and helped me learn how to sew from patterns and work with fabric and lining. I spotted a little discount fabric store and went to town! I ended up sewing many of my own drapes here in Atlanta—the swags, the rosettes, the whole deal. And now some of my home decor has been featured in magazines and on TV. Not bad for a lady who didn't used to know the difference between latex and oil paint.

WHAT I'VE LEARNED: The challenges you encounter when you aim high are the levers for moving you closer to your goals.

CONFIDENCE BOOSTER: Dream big! Sometimes all you need is a helping hand to show you how to achieve your goals. And a goal reached will make your confidence soar. Acknowledge the process of each victory with all of its challenges and support along the way. You need both!

THE POWER OF TEAMWORK

As my little story about the Murder in the Powder Room illustrates, there's nothing like teamwork for making your void your value and building confidence, whether it's with your spouse, your parents, your siblings, your school, your church, your coworkers, or your fellow athletes.

In fact, it's hard to think of someone who doesn't rely on a team at some point to achieve a goal or dream. I was so defeated in my initial DIY efforts that there's no way I would have gotten those walls in shape by myself. Without Tim to save the day, that whole weekend would have been a nightmare. And without Mom to show me how to sew drapes, I wouldn't have had pride in my handicrafts.

Being part of a team is a good place to start shoring up or jump-starting your own confidence.

Have you ever watched geese heading south for the winter? They fly in a V pattern. Know why? Each bird makes an updraft for the one behind it, so all the ones in the back get to conserve their energy. Then the birds in front fall to the back when they get tired, and as a group they fly farther before having to rest. Together, they supposedly get 70 percent farther than they would on their own.

That's what a team does. It works together toward one goal, to make it easier and better for every member.

As you begin to make your void your value and increase your confidence, don't be afraid to ask for help. There's no rule saying you have to do it all alone. And you may even reach your goal faster, which means a speedy jump start for your confidence!

The Takeaway

When you really want that dream, you'll put in the hard work to achieve it. And it won't seem like hard work because you love it so much. Instead of endeavoring to be a star or to make mega-millions, endeavor to do what you love! As you get more accomplished, the confidence will follow, and every step you'll be closer to living your dream!

Robin's Ramblings

"If you can't fly, then run. If you can't run, then walk. If you can't walk, then crawl. But whatever you do, you have to keep moving forward."

—*Dr. Martin Luther King Jr.*

16

THE CONFIDENCE TO BE A GOOD SPOUSE

Introducing . . . Crystal!

"Everyone else gets Robin, the hot news anchor lady. I get Crystal."

My husband made this remark to a roomful of people backstage at a country concert just this past weekend, where our buddies The Lost Trailers opened for country duo Montgomery Gentry. Then he went on to describe Crystal—his name for me when the makeup comes off and the slippers go on. (It's short for Crystal Meth and comes from what we imagine someone must look like after emerging from a two-day bender. My name for him, when he's in a similar love-me-as-I-am look, is Jack. Short for "Jack Daniel's.")

"Yeah, she's greasy-faced. Her hair's all FUBAR, and her morning breath knocks you into tomorrow."

The room fell out laughing.

He refers to me repeatedly as "Crystal" because he knows it makes me laugh.

WE NOW INTERRUPT OUR REGULARLY
SCHEDULED EDUCATION...

His humor has been a constant in our relationship ever since we met during my senior year of college. I was a transfer student from Malone College. It offered a concentration in broadcast journalism, but at the time it had no full-time operational TV broadcasting facility for hands-on learning. I had thought I was doing just fine in my education until I got my first internship.

It was in Washington, D.C.!

I was going to live in the Capitol Hill neighborhood!

I was going to intern at C-SPAN!

(Cue the slam-on-the-brakes sound, followed by crickets...)

C-SPAN?

Okay, it wasn't the most rockin' internship a person could have, but it provided a great foundation of knowledge of the way Congress works.

So when I got word, I packed up my big hair, little butt (now I have the opposite—my butt is big and my hair is not), and daily Cream of Wheat habit, and hauled my little hick self to the big city for a semester.

I first realized I might need to get more serious about my broadcasting studies when a fellow intern looked over from her desk. She said, "Isn't learning how to do stand-ups on camera hard? Man! It's tough to figure out what you want to say and how it's going to fit into your story!"

My reply amounted to, "Uh-huh, oh, definitely!" I had no idea what she was talking about! Stand-up? Sit down? Do the Hokey Pokey?

WRONG, said the buzzer.

That was the moment I realized my mostly book-and-theory-style education was not going to get the job done, if I was going to succeed in the cutthroat world of broadcast news, where the competition is F-I-E-R-C-E. I needed book, theory, political science, *and* on-air experience. So after I finished that internship that semester, I transferred to Ashland University, which Tim was already attending.

At the time Ashland had a great reputation for getting its grads into Ohio stations and beyond. My major there was radio/television programming, performance, and production. So why didn't I go there in the first place? Well, because the school also had a reputation for being expensive. And it was only about a half hour away from my hometown, and I didn't want my parents to make me stay home to save money. I wanted to *live* the college experience, not drive to it.

But as it turned out I got a scholarship, found a cheap efficiency apartment off campus, and didn't sign up for the meal plan. Add up all those discounts and penny-pinchings, and voilà! The price was about the same as for my old college. So I switched schools over Christmas.

I didn't know anybody when I got there. And since I wasn't interested in being in a sorority and I lived off campus, I wasn't into Ashland's social scene. I was a radio/television nerd. I practically camped out in the TV building, producing or hosting news shows, and cohosting and producing a once-a-week show called *Nightlife* with a live band and guests.

My life was so bereft of social activity that I didn't even realize that Joe Jock/Mr. Fraternity had been watching me from afar. When I first ran into him on the quad, my sympathetic heart noticed only his football injury, his crutches, and his minions escorting his every move.

Said I to him, "What happened to your leg?"

Said he to me, "What, you don't know? Everyone knows what happened to my leg."

Said I to myself, *What a jerk!* And thus a true love story began.

Tim says he spotted me on campus the year I transferred and thought I was a professor because I dressed up so much. But I dressed up because of my evening job as a reporter.

Tim kept trying to find out more about me and finally asked somebody in my political science class, "Hey, who is that?"

Then the next year we crossed paths a couple of times a week on campus, and he would always say, "Hi, Robin." I'd think, *How does that guy know my name?* I would also notice his smile. It was nice. To this day he has perfect teeth.

YIN AND YANG

One reason I fell in love with Tim was that he was so self-confident and supportive of my career aspirations. And he was totally willing to go into businesses that he could leave to follow me around the country.

We dated for three years and married in 1993 when I was working in Columbus. How big was the wedding? Humongous. He had ten attendants, and counting the three junior flower girls I had fourteen. Yep, that's twenty-four total. (I told him to have as many groomsmen as he needed to include all the people he wanted. So the big bridesmaid party was his idea.)

Not only that. We invited eight hundred guests, and six hundred showed. It was ridiculous! But that's what Tim wanted. Usually it's the woman who sets the pace for the wedding, right? But Tim thought of his hometown friends, family, and fraternity brothers, and he didn't want to leave anybody out. He was afraid he would hurt their feelings. Such a tender man!

Tim is the yin to my yang, the patience to my impatience. I probably would have chewed up, spit out, and worn out any other man within a week, given the demands of my career. How many men will seriously consider being a househusband? Tim actually stayed home for a while—without complaining, I might add!

Sometimes I felt bad about it. We went to his ten-year class reunion and people asked, "What are you doing now, Tim?" I'll never forget the looks on their faces when he said, "Right now, I stay home, because my wife has weird hours and we want to spend time together." You'd have thought he'd said, "I'm a beggar" or "I have a third nipple."

It's unfair, because in our society if a wife said she stayed home, no one would think twice. People would have thought, *Sure, she's making dinner and keeping the house.* And Tim did that. He would cook and have everything ready when I got home, pay all the bills, and keep the house and yard. Tim did it all. In the end, it wore on him. He'll tell you now that he felt much better about himself when he got out and opened a business.

That's not to say Tim's not very secure in his masculinity.

He's never had a problem with who brings home the bacon. It's always been one pot of gold, and that's one thing that's made our marriage work.

But I appreciate Tim for so much more than his willingness to be flexible with my job, this career, these hours. I love him for who he is. And I also think he's very handsome. First, he's got those teeth! That great dark hair. (No Grecian Formula for my guy!) And terrific skin that a proper face wash has never touched. (Actually, I don't think he even washes his face. I think it gets clean from whatever falls down from his head when he's shampooing. Lucky dog.)

Dale Carnegie wrote, "A person's name is to that person the sweetest and most important sound in any language." And the sweetest sound to me is *my* name...when *Tim* says it!

Here are my tips on being confident in marriage:

TIPS FOR BEING A CONFIDENT SPOUSE

1) First and foremost: Find humor in each other.

I tell young women who ask my advice about dating or marriage to look for the person who makes you laugh! Humor has been key in my marriage. Simply put, it's hard to stay mad at someone who is making you laugh!

Tim is talented at making me laugh at the silly things I do. But you have to find humor in yourself, too, in the mundane things you do, and in the absurd. Entertain each other! Tim likes to dare me to do the outrageous, and the currency for the bet is almost always some unattainable piece of jewelry.

Most recently he dared me to do the birthday suit salute as we cruised on a pontoon boat on the lake.

"How long?" I asked with a raise of the eyebrow.

"Sixty seconds," he said, half-fearing I might.

"What do I get?" I negotiated.

"A gargantuan ring."

I gave him one of those looks, and he shot back, "Nobody will see you."

Yeah, right. The lake we were visiting that weekend has so many people on it the Sunday traffic seems like the entire north side of Atlanta making its way back home.

"Tim, if someone gets a picture, my career is over."

He knows my career is the linchpin, the saving grace. Or else he'd be out a ton of money, because I'd win those bets!

Seriously, though, I tell other women, "Don't look for the guy who has the best muscles or the most money." Here's why: the looks go. The money can evaporate. And besides, since when does money mean love? It's the most ludicrous thought. If your mate goes bankrupt, then where are you?

Tim and I have always been astonished at women who marry for any reason other than love. How can a dollar amount equate to a relationship? That doesn't make you happy. Love is not an equation. Love is an emotion and a bond that is unconditional.

So let's talk about marrying for looks. I know someone's appearance may stop you in your tracks the first time you meet him. And he may take your breath away for a time. But let's not go marrying the arm candy, ladies. Those muscles are going to turn to flab sooner or later unless you're married to

Sly Stallone. That chiseled jaw stands a very good chance of drooping eventually. And so will *your* best features. *But funny lasts forever.*

Because believe you me, when you're seventy or eighty, you're going to want to be able to laugh. Your arguments won't be half as bad if your spouse can make you laugh at yourself.

2) Be happy.

Did you know happiness rubs off? It's been proven. We had a story on *Morning Express with Robin Meade* that explained scientifically how happiness is contagious. The study found that if you are around happy people, you are much more likely to be happy yourself. And the most unusual finding of that study is that your happiness can spread outward to social circles you're not even a part of! In other words, if you're happy, the emotion is so strong that you could not only make your spouse happy but make others happy through him! Fascinating!

The bottom line is that we're attracted to happy people. Don't you want your spouse to be attracted to you on an emotional level?

3) Show gratitude to each other.

Tim handles all the bills. He would tell you that I take that for granted, and I do. I wouldn't even begin to know where our checkbook is. I don't know what our house payment is. And I don't want to know. I'm the word lady. I'm not the numbers lady. But I do show gratitude toward him for those things, and for the little things, too. And he shows gratitude toward me. That's very important, because a lot of times in a marriage, you nag at each other:

"Tim, did you remember to take out the trash?"

"Well, no."

"Tim, did you call about the mosquito abatement program, since you're interested in that?"

"Not yet."

So I've found you've really got to balance the negatives in your marriage with positives, starting with gratitude.

And here's a little secret: the more you show thanks toward your significant other, the more that person will want to do things for you. Just like puppies, people love praise. That goes for your spouse, too.

4) Try not to bully or pick on your mate.

That's hard to remember when you're bickering. Tim is bad about play-bullying and picking on me after I've already keyed down for sleep. Because I get up so early for my job, I have to wind down much earlier than he does. Sometimes he hasn't even gotten home yet when I go to bed. But if he is home I'll say, "Come tuck me into bed. I'm in my jammies and I'm already in my Zen moment."

But sometimes he'll tease and poke me as you would a dog or a small child. I'll say, "I'm not your mother," because he and his brothers pull pranks on their mom and laugh at her reaction. So he needs to cool his jets on that one.

And I know he hates being pinched, so I don't do that to him, not even in an affectionate way. He also hates it if I roll my eyes at him. It sends him into a rage, because he thinks it means I'm belittling him. So I know to never roll my eyes when I'm trying to make a point.

5) Remember your spouse is the same person you stood with before the altar.

In other words, when you're feeling less than "in love," try to remember all those qualities you were so infatuated with before you got married. For example, my mom knows how to push my dad's buttons. And he gets all up in arms. He'll say to one of us kids, "Apparently I've done everything wrong today. Your mother is just yelling and cursing at me." But then the fact that she's a funny, entertaining little spitfire is also what attracted my father to her originally.

So when you and your spouse are fighting, ask yourself, *Is the person I fell in love with still inside there?* If you are a continuous being, isn't your mate continuous and still the same person you encountered all those years ago? It's hard to see sometimes, but worth the hunt.

6) Take pains to do things that please your mate.

Tim, for example, has treated me like a lady from day one. The first time I went to one of his fraternity parties, he went to great lengths to get me a six-pack of Diet Coke for the evening. I didn't drink and there weren't going to be any nonalcoholic drinks there. I thought, *What a gentleman! Very chivalrous.* He was very respectful and still is.

That same night, we were taking a break from our early-nineties dancing. We sat facing each other, and I noticed my hand fit perfectly in his. Then he said something that was so unusual for a twentyish frat guy: he looked at my long nails and lean fingers and said, "I just love your hands." How many young men say that? Turns out he'd always admired the way his grandmother kept her nails manicured and painted and even went so far as to say he could never date a woman with masculine hands. Ha! I try to keep my hands looking nice for him today.

7) Try to keep up your appearance for each other, and don't be stingy with the compliments.

Men are said to be visually oriented, so try to look good for your mate. I don't mean you should wake up with a face full of makeup or shouldn't wear sweats around the house. But do try to stay healthy. That directly affects how you feel about yourself. It also directly affects your intimacy, because if you don't feel good about yourself, then you're not going to want to make someone else feel good.

I compliment Tim on his looks all the time. To this day I'll see him and think, *He just dresses so well.* And when he has on a handsome outfit, I'll tell him. I want him to do the same for me.

I always say to him, "I don't care what other people think about how I look, but I do care about how *you* think I look." Because I want him to say, "There's the woman I fell in love with when she was twenty-three, and I can still see why I did."

8) Know when to employ the fine art of the freak-out!

You can help your spouse feel confident he truly knows what's important to you by employing the fine art of the freak-out. The freak-out must be used sparingly, as the more often you use it the less impact it will have. Ready? Tim has attention-deficit tendencies (whether he actually has that disorder has never been diagnosed), so he checks out mentally every now and then. It's aggravating in a relationship. I'll say, "But I told you I need this."

"No, I don't remember that. You never said that."

"Yes, honey, I did. Remember, I was standing right over there?"

"No."

But he does run three companies in that brain of his, and that's pretty impressive. Still, every now and then I've got to have a big freak-out to make a point. For example:

Last summer we were out on the boat and thought we'd go down to the marina to get a late breakfast. Well, they were swamped, and they said they weren't going to seat anybody for a half hour. So I said to Tim, "Let's just get out of here."

We got back home and started playing around on the Jet Ski, and it got late and we still hadn't eaten. So I went into the kitchen about two or three o'clock, and I made a big salad with tomatoes and strawberries and cucumbers. It was a busy salad, and I was really happy with it. And Tim came in when I was just facedown in the bowl. Truly. My lips were not far from the bottom of the bowl, because it was just a lot more convenient to get that last morsel, right?

I was barely coming up for air, and he went, "Damn, baby! Are you pregnant or something? You got cravings?"

And I roared up like a Jurassic monster, replete with sound effects. "What? No! I'm eating salad. *Salad!* If I were pregnant, don't you think I'd be eating something better than *salad*?"

And then he came over to try to love up on me, and I said, "Don't you touch me! It was *salad*!"

It's comical now. But he got the point, and I bet you ten bucks he doesn't say that again.

The worst "Damn, baby!" moment occurred when we lived in Miami. I was really good at staying thin then. I basically didn't eat "cheater"-type foods during the week (your pastas, pizzas, and pies), and then I ate whatever I wanted on the weekends. (Nothing I recommend as healthy today, now that I know a lot more about how our bodies work.)

One weekend evening it was really hot. I said to Tim, "Let's go to TCBY and get some frozen yogurt." (For years I had this thing for frozen yogurt. In my mind I could eat it, and eat it, and eat it, and it wasn't bad for me, and I wasn't sinning. Of course, it's still sugar. It's still calories. But you couldn't tell me that then.)

So we went to TCBY, and I got in line and said, "I'll have a large waffle cone with raspberries on top." Now, when they pour that thing, it's huge. They handed it to me, and Tim said—no, he LOUDLY EXCLAIMED—in front of this huge crowd, "Damn, baby!"

At those words, all the people beside us at the counter swiveled their heads my way simultaneously, as if they were watching a ball at a tennis match. Even the workers at the counter craned their necks around to see who was bellying up to the yogurt bar.

And you know what Tim did? He laughed and giggled! *Giggled!* I suppose the "Damn, baby!" comment was funny in his Guy Brain. But it was *not* funny in my Gal Brain. I wanted to crawl under a rock. He says today I'd just had a big dinner, and that's why he said it. I don't remember. But in my mind, there's always room for frozen yogurt, and it was hot, and it was Miami. So I was ticked off. And I snapped, *"Don't you ever say that to me again in front of people! It's frozen yogurt, for Pete's sake!"* And he said, "Whoa!"

So every now and then I think a freak-out is good. It forces your mate to come out of his or her ADD moment and realize, *Oh, this really matters to her! I'm pretty confident this is a point she wanted me to "get."*

THE JENNA JAMESON INCIDENT...
BOWW CHICKA-BOWW BOWW

Having confidence in your mate, especially in his sexual fidelity, is paramount to a happy marriage. But self-confidence is also a gift for both partners in any union. It's hard to prescribe how to be self-confident, but it really does help if each of you is secure in your masculinity or femininity and how it fits into your relationship. That way you'll engender trust in one another, and you probably won't smother each other with suspicion.

Take, for example, what Tim and I call the Jenna Jameson Incident.

I was at a bowling outing on a Friday night, and called to ask Tim, "Why don't you pick me up after bowling?" I thought he could bring Lexa, one of our two German shepherds at the time (the other, Rocco, was in training), and then we could drive to the lake directly afterward.

Tim drove into the parking lot about 8:30 p.m., and some of the guys I was bowling with came outside all charged up. One of them said, "Hey, I saw a sign that said Jenna Jameson is appearing down the street. Let's go!" And Tim said, "I can't. We're on our way to the lake house." I said, "Oh, Tim, you go ahead. I'll be right here with Lexa. I've got some e-mails to do on the BlackBerry, and we'll just take a little nap until you guys come back."

One guy was like, "Man! She's letting you go see a porn star at a dance spot? My wife would kick my ass."

Oh, come on, it's not as if they were starring in the taping of a porn DVD. They were just going to check out her event, whatever it was. So I said, "I don't care. He can look all he wants. He just can't touch. Besides, I know who he's coming back to."

Well, as it turned out, Tim came back sooner than I expected. The other fellas looked all deflated, their heads down, hands in their pockets, like mopey kids kicking cans in the street. Why? Those dudes trudged all the way down there only to discover that Jenna Jameson wasn't at a dance spot at all. The sign was at a *bookstore*, and she was going to be appearing there to *sign her book* in a month or so. That was one disappointed group of red-blooded boys!

Later, on the drive, Tim and I talked about it all, and he said, "Everyone thinks you're the coolest wife. But the truth is you have people e-mailing you every day saying they love you. So you have abnormal self-confidence because of your viewers."

If so, it works in both our favors, because Tim seems happy being married to me. Ha!

Oh, don't let him kid you—he loves the bragging rights on this next one: in 2004, the readers of *Playboy* magazine's website named me "Sexiest Newscaster." I had 40 percent of the vote, or 16,145 votes out of a total of 40,380. Whee-whoo! The margin had never been so large.

At the time, however, the public-relations folks at CNN seemed mortified. I could understand they wouldn't want me known as "the *Playboy* anchor." They wanted to know what I thought.

Well, these were my thoughts: "Hey, at least it's not the 'News Anchor You'd Least Like to Meet in a Dark Alley' award. I don't care why people are watching, as long as they are watching!"

If only the Playboy.com voters could see Crystal, right?!

The Takeaway

Recently I told my husband how sexy his confidence is to me. I told him his lack of jealousy was attractive—he didn't become suspicious at my every move or turn green if I held a conversation with a man as handsome as he. His response: "Thank you for conducting yourself in a way that makes me confident!"

In other words, we are both confident in our relationship, and confident in ourselves as individuals. We try to make sure we're not giving off signals or acting as if we're hunting for someone else to fill that special role. We've watched some of our married friends get into trouble because one of them flirted, sending mixed signals to people of the opposite sex.

While no physical transgressions may take place in these

situations, the emotional harm such flirting can do to your partner's ego and self-confidence could put a question mark in his or her heart forever. Give your mate a reason to feel confident about your union, and don't give him or her a reason to doubt it.

Robin's Ramblings

Don't let anyone frighten you with their stories or their experience: marriage is a good thing, if you make it a good thing. Be confident that you can!

A NOTE FROM
THE AUTHOR

You may have picked up this book because you feel your confidence could use a boost. You hoped you could glean some nuggets of information from this person whose position requires her to do her job in front of many eyeballs every morning. Because of the public nature of my job, you assumed I had some insights into the challenge of keeping, getting, or maintaining self-confidence. If you were indeed looking for insight on how to walk into the house of confidence, I hope this book has encouraged you to at least crack the door! Through frank anecdotes from my life, I've tried to lay bare some of the issues I've had to work with in my own view of self.

Today, at HLN, I've done a complete 180 from my confidence-challenged days. I'm comfortable in nearly any situation on air. I wear whatever clothes I choose. I'm not afraid to be the dissenting voice in discussions with coworkers. When appropriate, I don't mind voicing my opinion with you, the viewer. In other words, I've found my confidence.

You might think I'm a suck-up when you read this next part, but I'm telling you, a lot of credit for this change in me should go to my current and previous bosses at HLN. They praise authenticity and the quality of being relatable. These are not pointy-heads who dictate: "Be like so and so over on that other channel!" "Do something with your hair!" "Curtail your jubilance."

In other words, I am not pressured to be a typical news anchor. And I'm not typical, anyway. I'm irreverent at times. I favor big necklaces that some say rival Mr. T's. I wear sweaters instead of stiff business suits. I like to pull back the curtain, so to speak, to let viewers see what's going on behind the scenes at the newsroom—even if there's a chance they might see our warts.

When it comes to the formula for success, everyone's is different. But here's the deal: all of us are born with the potential to do great things. Somewhere along the line you've allowed someone or something to convince you otherwise. In reality you have abilities, talents, and potential, just as everyone else has.

My eighth-grade English teacher said to us on the first day of school, "Right now, you all are starting out with A's." In other words, it was up to us what we'd do with our A's, whether we'd continue to earn them or do something to lose them. Likewise, you, at your center, start out with an A in life and confidence. So if you're lacking in self-confidence, you're not tuned in to what you have to offer.

Don't lowball your own capabilities. Don't underestimate your own abilities. Try to look at yourself in an unbiased and impartial way. For me, the key has been to really peer into myself and look for my misconceptions about myself and about other people.

I hope this book in some way has helped start you on a path to real self-evaluation and self-appreciation—and genuine, lasting confidence!

To maintain your confidence, you must continually take stock of your abilities and contributions to keep your view of yourself a realistic one. And you must remember that your view of yourself in turn becomes your view of the world. If you have faith in yourself, you will ultimately have faith in people around you and believe the world is a good place where you can thrive and contribute. This is my hope for you!

I wish you all the best on your personal journey. And may all the news in your life be good!

—Robin

ACKNOWLEDGMENTS

First, to the viewer and reader: thank you!

In the "book world":

Thank you to Sarah Sper, who approached me to write this book. Thank you to executive editor Michelle Rapkin for taking on this project as your own, during a very difficult time in your life. May you always have fond memories of your Bob when you see this book. Mel Berger at William Morris—thank you for seeing me through this as my literary agent, and for your frank appraisal. I'm honored! Thanks, Alanna Nash, for your work. To Gina Wynn, Center Street sales director, and the entire sales team—what fun is writing if nobody gets to see it? Thanks for getting my work into the hands of the people! To marketing director Pamela Clements, marketing manager Preston Cannon, and publicity director Jana Burson: I shall call you three "the trinity of marketing and publicity"—thanks for your innate knowledge that books are not bought, they are sold (a phrase I'll borrow from the aforementioned Mel Berger). Each of you three is a gem! Thank you, everyone at Center Street Books and Hachette!

In the "television world":

To Ken Jautz, executive vice president of CNN Worldwide, thank you for being enthusiastic about this project from the first mention of it. Bill Galvin, vice president of HLN, I'm so grateful for the atmosphere you foster at HLN, where we can take our jobs seriously, but not ourselves. Thank you for being behind this all the way! Executive producer Steve Rosenberg, senior producer Susan Jalali, senior producer Nima Ahmed, senior producer Janye McClinton, and the entire producing/writing/editing/technical/directorial team on *Morning Express with Robin Meade*: you make work not seem like work! Your dedication, skill, and enthusiasm are the stuff of dreams. Thank you to the people on air with me everyday: Bob, Jennifer, Rafer, and Richard. You rock! Janine Iamunno—you are the PR guru! To all of the CNN/HLN PR team: many many thanks! Chief marketing officer Scot Safon, Jennifer Boardman and Lara Hurst in CNN Strategic Marketing, and Kate Swenson in CNN Strategic Marketing Interactive, your work is inspiring! To CNN promotions folks, thank you for letting the world know about this book. Thank you very much, Pollyanna Dunn. Noni Gibbs, executive administrative assistant: you're a lifesaver. Thank you, Jim Walton, president of CNN Worldwide, for being the leader of this huge machine we call

Cable News Network. Ken Lindner, my TV agent, and his outstanding staff at Ken Lindner and Associates, thank you for believing and for all the work you've done through the years. Thank you to the viewers who allow me into their homes to start the day. If it weren't for you, I wouldn't have a job, hah!

In my "family world":
My parents, Linny and Sharon: I love you dearly. Thank you for…well…EVERYTHING, from the moment I was born, to the woman I am today! For all your sacrifices, for all the family experiences that make up the backbone of this book, and for your guidance. Thank you to my sister and brother, Tonda and Kevin, for allowing me to mention you in this book and share stories from our childhood. I love you! Thank you to my in-laws for your love and applause all these years. My nieces and nephews in descending order of age: Heather, Carl, Paige, Karley, Kathleen, Blake, Cade, and Cole: Aunt Robbie will always think the sun rises and sets with you! I love you! Godchild Ava, her sister Sofie, and little Jack, too: I hope you always feel confident to chase your dreams.

Finally, Dr. Case: you inspire me each time we talk. Thank you for your knowledge. I hope this writing does it justice. And Tim: thank you for you. I love our life together, and I love you! Hope you're up for the next fifteen years of this exhilarating roller-coaster ride we call marriage! You are my sunshine.

ABOUT THE AUTHOR

ROBIN MEADE is the anchor of HLN's morning show *Morning Express with Robin Meade*. Among other stories, Meade anchored the network's coverage of the wars in Afghanistan and Iraq, the January 2009 inauguration of President Barack Obama, and the July 2009 coverage of Michael Jackson's memorial event. In July 2008, she scored the exclusive first interview with freed American hostages—at their request—after their release from Fuerzas Armadas Revolucionarias de Colombia (FARC) captors. In June 2009, Meade performed a tandem skydive with President George Herbert Walker Bush in Kennebunkport, Maine, to commemorate President Bush's eighty-fifth birthday. Meade is also the face of HLN's "Salute to Troops" segment, a daily message to U.S. troops using photos and videos sent in by their loved ones.

Before joining CNN, Meade worked at NBC Chicago affiliate WMAQ-TV, and held anchor positions at WSVN-TV's *Today in Florida* in Miami, WCMH-TV in Columbus, Ohio, and at WJW-TV in Cleveland. Meade began her career in broadcasting at WMFD-TV in Mansfield, Ohio, where she worked as a reporter.

Meade is based at CNN's world headquarters in Atlanta, where she lives with her husband, Tim, and their cat and two dogs.

Eat Sweat Play

Anna Kessel is a sports writer for the *Guardian* and the *Observer*. She is also the co-founder and chair of Women in Football. In 2016 she received an MBE for her services to women in sport.